"Piper's story is astounding and his life lessons are real: Focus on the eternal, find the humor, accept help, give thanks, and just hold on."

—*Publishers Weekly*

"*Heaven Is Real* will encourage you to move beyond your past and discover what God has next for you. [You] will be reminded that the very things you wished had never happened in your life can actually become your greatest opportunities."

—Dr. Charles Redmond, senior pastor,
First Baptist Church, Pasadena, Texas

"[When] I met Don Piper in person, and heard him recount his experience to our congregation, I had no doubt this man had been to heaven. The reason . . . is how he now lives his life on earth. Indelible lessons were learned throughout that experience, which has changed him forever. As you read *Heaven Is Real*, you will discover that you don't need to go to heaven to learn these lessons, you simply need to listen to a man who has."

—Dr. Kevin M. Brennan, senior pastor,
Evangel Church, Scotch Plains, New Jersey

"Don Piper is an ordinary man with an extraordinary experience and calling . . . This book will lift your eyes from the trials and troubles of this life and warm your heart as you realize that everything you do here on earth can make a difference for eternity."

—Gregg Harris, president,
Far East Broadcasting Company

"In this book, Don tells the story—more than life overcoming death, more than stories of faith and fear—but the story of faith and love and hope and grace of Christ. This is the story of every Christian who has invested in his hope and his grace. Be prepared to be blessed!"

—Ron Hill, senior pastor,
The Fellowship of San Antonio

Berkley Praise titles by
Don Piper and Cecil Murphey

HEAVEN IS REAL

DAILY DEVOTIONS INSPIRED BY 90 MINUTES IN HEAVEN

Lessons on Earthly Joy—What
Happened After *90 Minutes in Heaven*

Heaven Is Real

Don Piper

and Cecil Murphey

BERKLEY PRAISE, NEW YORK

THE BERKLEY PUBLISHING GROUP
Published by the Penguin Group
Penguin Group (USA) Inc.
375 Hudson Street, New York, New York 10014, USA
Penguin Group (Canada), 90 Eglinton Avenue East, Suite 700, Toronto, Ontario M4P 2Y3, Canada
(a division of Pearson Penguin Canada Inc.)
Penguin Books Ltd., 80 Strand, London WC2R 0RL, England
Penguin Group Ireland, 25 St. Stephen's Green, Dublin 2, Ireland (a division of Penguin Books Ltd.)
Penguin Group (Australia), 250 Camberwell Road, Camberwell, Victoria 3124, Australia
(a division of Pearson Australia Group Pty. Ltd.)
Penguin Books India Pvt. Ltd., 11 Community Centre, Panchsheel Park, New Delhi—110 017, India
Penguin Group (NZ), 67 Apollo Drive, Rosedale, North Shore 0632, New Zealand
(a division of Pearson New Zealand Ltd.)
Penguin Books (South Africa) (Pty.) Ltd., 24 Sturdee Avenue, Rosebank, Johannesburg 2196,
South Africa

Penguin Books Ltd., Registered Offices: 80 Strand, London WC2R 0RL, England

PRINTING HISTORY
Berkley Praise hardcover edition / August 2008
Berkley Praise trade paperback edition / January 2009

Berkley Praise trade paperback ISBN: 978-0-425-22646-9

The Library of Congress has catalogued the Berkley Praise hardcover as follows:

Piper, Don, 1950–
    Heaven is real : lessons on earthly joy—what happened after 90 minutes in heaven / Don Piper and
Cecil Murphey.—1st ed.
        p. cm.
    Includes bibliographical references.
    ISBN-13: 978-0-425-21555-5
    1. Heaven—Christianity.   I. Murphey, Cecil B.   II. Title.
    BT846.3.P57 2007
    236'.24—dc22

                                                                                        2007011989

PRINTED IN THE UNITED STATES OF AMERICA

10 9 8 7 6 5 4 3 2 1

Scripture identified as

*   are taken from the King James Version of the Bible. Copyright © 1979, 1980, 1982 by Thomas
       Nelson, Inc., Publishers.

**   are taken from the *Holy Bible*, New Living Translation, copyright © 1996. Used by permission of
       Tyndale House Publishers, Inc., Wheaton, Illinois 60189. All rights reserved.

***   are taken from *The Message*. Copyright © 1993, 1994, 1995, 1996, 2000, 2001, 2002. Used by
       permission of NavPress Publishing Group.

†   are taken from the *Holy Bible*, New International Version. Copyright © 1973, 1978, 1984 In-
       ternational Bible Society. Used by permission of Zondervan Bible Publishers.

The publisher does not have any control over and does not assume any responsibility for author or
third-party websites or their content.

CONTENTS

Contents

ACKNOWLEDGMENTS

You now hold the book I've wanted to write since I spent a sleepless night on the twenty-first floor of St. Luke's Medical Center in 1989. After a traumatic car accident that gave me a glimpse of glory, morning sunrise signaled the first day of the rest of my life. But I wasn't ready to write it.

Friends and family had to convince me to tell that part of the story. They said it would help others. It still took me fourteen years to put that heavenly experience on paper. *90 Minutes in Heaven: A True Story of Death and Life* chronicles my trip to heaven and my miraculous return to earth.

Since the publication of that first book, I have spoken worldwide and received thousands of e-mails, letters, and phone calls. I have heard countless personal testimonies. All of those responses have borne out the ministry of that book. During that time, I also introduced the subject dearest to my heart: I call it "The New Normal." I can write about the new normal because I know with total certainty that heaven *is* real.

Acknowledgments

In the years following my accident, friends and relatives forced me to find a purposeful way to live after tragedy and loss. Many self-revelations about that journey appear in this book— lessons on earthly joy learned from spending ninety minutes in heaven.

I have prayed and will continue to pray that this book will be as helpful to those seeking life after loss as others have found my first book. Heaven is real and we can go there some- day. Until then, God wants us to experience a meaningful life on earth.

This heartfelt project would not have been possible without my gifted writing partner, Cecil Murphey. Cec is a dear friend and one of the premier wordsmiths of our time. And he knows inti- mately what it is like to live the new normal. Our agent, Deidre Knight, of the Knight Agency is a joy to both of us. From the be- ginning, she sensed that this project would touch many lives. Our editor, Denise Silvestro, tirelessly polished this manuscript to make sure that it does touch lives. Thank you, Cec, Deidre, and Denise, for your faith and support.

People from every corner of the globe have inspired me on my journey. Their encouragement has given me my new normal. My life has been blessed because of my daughter, Nicole; my sons, Chris and Joe; and my wife, Eva. I am privileged to have my par- ents, Billie and Ralph, and my in-laws, Eldon and Ethel Pente- cost, support my journey.

I dedicate this book to those mentioned above and to ev- eryone who has turned tragedies into testimonies, disappoint-

Acknowledgments

ments into divine appointments, desperation into inspiration, and losses into victories.

Heaven is real.

—Don Piper
March 2007

Heaven Is Real

ONE

I Cross the Bridge

Heaven is real. I know it because I have been there and back. As strange as that may sound, it's true. As much as I can communicate with words, I want to share that experience and the aftermath—especially to write about the things I learned. The problem is that no one can explain an experience so perfectly that everyone can feel it exactly as it happened. I can only try.

My story began January 18, 1989.

Crossing the bridge over Lake Livingston, in Texas, changed my life forever. That was the day I died and went to heaven. It was *not* a near-death experience: I literally died. Two EMTs, and possibly as many as eight, examined my lifeless body and pronounced me dead after an eighteen-wheeler mangled my Ford Escort with me inside. Unable to get me out of the vehicle, they covered my car with a tarp.

After the impact, I didn't see light or float through a tunnel. I didn't undergo anything like what is described by those who have had a near-death experience (NDE). One second I was alive, and the next instant, I stood at the gates of heaven. I make a point of this because some people can't believe that any person could go to heaven and return (except Jesus). They insist I only had a near-death experience. I don't argue with them, but I know I died. I went to heaven and I experienced the awe, the joy, and the utter perfection of the life that awaits all of God's people.

I do want to make a brief explanation about my death. First, one fact is irrefutable: I showed no signs of life for at least ninety minutes. Those with NDEs are out of their bodies for a few minutes at most; I was out for at least an hour and a half.

Human bodies contain about six quarts (5.6 liters) of blood. I had wounds all over my body. If it had been an NDE, my heart would have continued to pump blood. If I had not died, my heart would have continued to beat. In that case, I would have bled out—my heart would have pumped blood until I died.

Because I was killed instantly, my heart stopped beating, and therefore, it didn't pump blood. No blood gushed out because no heart pumped it. If my heart had continued to pump, I would have lost so much blood that no matter what they did to try to save me, it would have made no difference because there would have been no way to replace that much fluid.

Second, I had no vital signs. The EMTs would have known the difference. They were professionals and used a portable EKG and said I had no measurable pulse. Most people know that if the brain is deprived of oxygen for more than six minutes, the brain cells die and the person can never be resuscitated. For at least an hour and a half, I showed *no* vital signs. When I returned to earth, I had lost little blood, and doctors found no evidence of brain damage.

I died.

That's the only sensible and logical way to explain what happened to me. Not only do I believe I died, but during my death, I experienced heaven. I had read about heaven in my Bible, heard sermons, and had absorbed a lot of theological teaching about life after this life. But none of those descriptions did justice to the real heaven.

How could they? Heaven is greater and more wonderful than human words can express. In my two previous books,[1] I gave details of my journey.

This book isn't about my journey *to* heaven; it's about my journey back *toward* heaven. By that, I mean I've been there once and now not only do I want to return, but I'm already on the road that will lead me back.

What I can share is that I'm different today than I was when I started across the bridge over Lake Livingston. That bridge changed my life. If I had not chosen to go over the bridge, I would not have the physical handicaps and the pain I experience today. But, then, I wouldn't have tasted the joys of heaven, either.

In the years since that accident I've often thought about bridges. They connect one place with another. They become the means by which we leave an old location and arrive in a new place. I've also come to think of bridges as symbols or metaphors to explain my life.

In this book, I've used the image of a bridge as my connecting point between drastic changes in life. We have many such bridges:

---

[1] *90 Minutes in Heaven: A True Story of Death and Life* by Don Piper with Cecil Murphey (Grand Rapids: Revell, 2004) and *Daily Devotions Inspired by 90 Minutes in Heaven* by Don Piper and Cecil Murphey (New York: Berkley Praise, 2006).

- the first day we entered school
- the day we graduated from high school or college
- the moment we held a driver's license in our hands
- when we heard the voice say, "You're hired" (or "You're fired")
- when we stared into the face of the person we loved and said, "I do"
- the realization of the loss of a close friend, parent, or loved one
- The dissolution of a marriage or a friendship.

The list goes on, but such experiences have one common factor: From that moment on, our lives shift direction. We may have worried or projected how we'd feel or the way we'd respond, but we never know what life is like on the other side of the viaduct until we get there.

After we've crossed such bridges, the old way is gone and we'll never be exactly the same. We may want to go back—and especially if that passage has taken us to a period of loss or pain—but there is no going back.

Crossing bridges also reminds us that life isn't always easy, and nowhere does God promise that it will be. We eagerly anticipate the happy, joyful times; we also have to face the sad, negative moments. For the upbeat times, we don't need or want advice on how to enjoy the incident. But when the bridge takes us into downbeat moments, most of us need a hand to grab or a shoulder to embrace.

In thinking about such transition points in our lives—and they *are* transitions—we need to see that life can never be the way it was before. We also need to realize that if they're sad or negative experiences, we can grow during those times.

Just before the completion of this book, my cowriter, Cecil Murphey, went through a harrowing experience. His home burned to the ground and his son-in-law died in the fire.

Not only did Cec lose someone he loved, but the fire destroyed all his material possessions. "I didn't like what happened," he said, "but I sensed God being with me through it all. Because of God's peace, I was able to face the losses and regain my emotional balance."

That example also reminds us that most of the time, we don't choose the bridges we cross. The best we can do at times is look to God's grace to help us with the transition.

Although we make many shifts in life, in this book I have focused on three specific bridges in my life. When I review my life as a whole, these three stand out as the most significant I can expect to face.

The bridges you face in your life may not be the same, but I assure you that one thing will be similar: You will experience life-altering change—we all do. You will come to a point in life where your world is turned upside down and nothing is the same. You won't be able to go back to the way things were; you will have to find a "new normal."

That's how crossing life's bridges works. At first, and perhaps for a long time, you may feel off-balance or disoriented but during that time Jesus Christ promises, "Peace I leave with you; my peace I give you. I do not give to you as the world gives. Do not let your hearts be troubled and do not be afraid" (John 114:27+).

The first significant bridge for me wasn't the bridge over Lake Livingston. I crossed a symbolic bridge at age sixteen. Even though I had no way to know it then, a conscious choice I made as a teenage boy altered the path I would travel through life. If I hadn't made that choice, I would never have been at a conference at Trinity Pines. If I hadn't crossed that bridge at age sixteen, I would never have gone to heaven, no matter when I died.

Here is the story of the first and most significant bridge I crossed.

I grew up in Bossier City, Louisiana, a city across the river from Shreveport. One summer afternoon when I was sixteen years old, the doorbell rang. My mother went to the front door and I heard her ask, "Who?" She turned around and called, "Don, there are three kids here to see you."

I went to the door and there stood a boy and two girls. They introduced themselves as Barry, Carmen, and Jan.

"We're from the First Baptist Church here in Bossier City," Barry said. One of the girls went to the same high school as I did, but the other two attended a rival school across town. They didn't tell me how they knew my name and I didn't think to ask.

"We've come here because we'd like to invite you to our church," Barry said.

I must have hesitated, because one of the girls asked, "Do you go to church?"

"No, I don't," I said and shook my head. "I mean, not regularly."

"Would you like to come to our church? We'd love to have you come," Barry said.

"We have a lot of activities for teens," one girl said.

"And we have a lot of fun doing things," the other said.

I knew First Baptist was a big church, even though I had not been there in years. "Uh, where do you meet?"

Enthusiastically they told me where they met and detailed many of their activities. "If you come we'll be there to greet you," all three of them promised.

"Yeah, okay," I said, and they gave me the times for all their meetings. Within five minutes they were gone. I didn't think much about their coming or my promise. But my parents had taught me that when I make a promise I should keep it. I had my driver's license, so it was an excuse to drive my car.

I don't think they expected me to visit their church, but I did. I parked in the parking lot and walked to the door they had mentioned. After I stepped inside, I saw it was some kind of greeting center. An older man directed me to the large room where the teens met.

As soon as I walked into the room, all three of them saw me, squealed in delight, and rushed up to me. I went to that church because they had invited me and I promised them I would be there. It was just that simple. I wouldn't have gone otherwise. I also went because three people invited me and said they'd be there to greet me so I wouldn't feel out of place.

Immediately I felt at home. I had somebody to sit with, and at age sixteen, no kid wants to sit alone or feel isolated. I went back the following Sunday and the one after that. Before long, Barry and I became good friends. I dated Jan a few times, and it wasn't long before I became a regular part of the youth fellowship.

The most important result of my going to youth activities was that I listened to what the Sunday school teachers had to say. I went to the worship services and no one put any pressure on me. When I asked questions, leaders answered me and no one condescended or treated me like some dumb kid. Frequently the adults and the other teens talked about being saved or being born again, but no one ever pressured me to have such an experience. Over a period of weeks, I came to the conclusion that I needed to make some changes. I didn't understand everything but I wanted to be different—I wanted that glow, that excitement for life that many of my born-again friends had. I thought about that for a couple of weeks, not sure how to proceed or even totally sure I wanted to change.

One Sunday morning, the pastor ended the service, as he did every week, with an invitation to us to turn to Jesus Christ. "God is calling you. Today's your day."

I knew God was calling me, but I didn't go forward; I didn't make a decision that day to follow Jesus Christ. I didn't resist because I was being obstinate, but I wanted to be sure I understood all I needed to do to become a Christian. I didn't want to leap into some kind of commitment and then ask, "What did I get myself into?" I wanted to understand what God expected of me.

I continued to ask questions. After one lengthy session of questions and answers, my Sunday school teacher said, "Why don't you invite the youth minister to your house and you can sit down and ask all the questions you want?"

"That's a great idea," I said.

At my invitation, our youth minister, Tom Cole, came to visit me two days later.

He was a friendly man and we talked sports, school, and other things teens usually discuss. After a few minutes, he leaned forward and asked, "Don, have you given much thought to becoming a Christian?"

"I've given a lot of thought to that. That's why I wanted you to come here."

He smiled and wisely waited for me to continue.

"Uh, see, I've gone to Sunday school and church for a couple of months now, and I've started to read the Bible—I read it regularly. I'm trying to understand."

He nodded.

"I'm just not sure what I need to do."

"It's really a simple process. If you believe—"

"I believe," I said.

"You ask Jesus Christ into your heart. You accept what he did for you on the cross." He explained the process of salvation slowly, patiently, and made sure I understood everything he said.

I nodded each time. The way he explained things made sense.

"Would you like to do that right now?"

"Yes, I would," I said, without the slightest hesitation. "I really would like to do that right now."

"Bow your head and ask Jesus into your heart."

It was just that simple. I prayed and asked Jesus Christ to come into my life and to save me. I prayed, as I learned later, what is often referred to as the sinner's prayer.

After I finished, both of us said, "Amen," and then he added, "The angels in heaven are rejoicing over this decision. They're singing your name because they know you're born into the kingdom of God."

I liked that thought and he opened the Bible and asked me to read aloud the words of Jesus: ". . . there is joy in the presence of the angels of God over one sinner that repenteth" (Luke 15:10*).

The sinner's prayer began my spiritual life. I had no idea that one decision, made at age sixteen, would change me and give my life direction. I knew that turning to God was important, but how could I have realized that everything in my world would change, especially my attitude and my values?

The years passed. My life evolved and I matured. I became more active in the church, went to college and seminary, and entered the ministry.

Because of that decision made at age sixteen, at age thirty-eight I attended a ministers' conference. When I was leaving the conference, I pulled up to the gate of Trinity Pines to turn on to the highway and put my foot on the brake for a few seconds before I drove through. In those few seconds I made another decision that would again change the course of my life.

The decision at sixteen determined where I went when I died in the car accident. At the time, I didn't realize that I had crossed the first and the most important bridge in my life. That decision to cross the bridge from eternal death to eternal life meant I would never be the same again. When I crossed my second bridge twenty-two years later, I was ready for heaven.

TWO

The Day I Turned Right

As I was leaving the conference at Trinity Pines, I made a simple decision. I turned right instead of left—the direction I usually went. It didn't seem like a big thing, at least not then. The conference had concluded a few minutes early so instead of leaving after lunch, I was off of the grounds shortly after 11:30 A.M.

When I reached the gates of Trinity Pines I paused. I don't know why. I simply thought, I'm not in a particular hurry today. I was supposed to give the Bible study at our church that night, but I had plenty of time.

Every other time I had been to Trinity Pines, I had turned left to go home by way of Livingston. If I turned right, I would drive through Huntsville on Texas Highway 19 and the road eventually bisects Lake Livingston. It was a route I had never taken before.

Only days before the conference I had received a traffic ticket for not wearing my seat belt. I saw the ticket on the passenger's seat and that reminded me to click it. I pulled forward, saw that the road was clear, and turned right. In 1989, the road just before the lake was narrow with no shoulders and no railings. Across the lake spanned a large, narrow bridge.

As I drove along, I knew the bridge was ahead. However, because of the overcast, I was fairly close before I spotted it. As I started across, I wondered why the government would construct a bridge like that in the middle of nowhere. It looked like a bridge I'd see in a major city with a metal superstructure, like the old ones that cross the rivers in downtown Minneapolis or Pittsburgh.

I slowed down and read a plaque that said the bridge had been built in the 1930s by the Works Progress Administration to put men to work during the Great Depression. It also read, "This bridge honors those who served in the Great War." Of course that referred to World War I.

I couldn't see beyond the end of the bridge because of an embankment. While I was still about thirty feet from the end, an eighteen-wheeler tractor trailer truck rushed toward me. I didn't know it at the time, but the truck, driven by a trustee from a nearby prison, was followed by a vehicle with prison guards.

The driver supposedly swerved to miss a car in his lane. By doing so, he hit my Ford and rolled over it. Nine wheels of that truck crushed my car and shoved it against the railing.

I died instantly.

Everything I relate about what happened after the accident was told to me by various witnesses. I wasn't there, I was dead, so I have to accept their accounts.

The prison guards immediately called for backup. Within minutes, four ambulances came to the scene of the accident because there were four vehicles involved in the wreck. So as far as I know, most of the eight EMTs examined me and pronounced me dead. The people in the other two cars were taken away. Their cars were disabled, but no one was hurt. Guards took the trustee back to prison.

Four sets of EMTs did a variety of tests on me, including an EKG. I was dead and I no longer bled, even though I had massive gaping wounds.

My car no longer had windows and my crushed body was clearly visible inside the crushed Ford. A number of bystanders had gathered and gaped at me. It was raining and a police officer found a tarp and covered my car. Traffic had backed up and they didn't want to encourage any additional rubbernecking.

Most of the traffic from the east—the direction from which I came—consisted of people who had also been at the conference. Two of those people were Dick and Anita Onarecker.

With the traffic backed up, Dick got out of his car, walked in the rain to the scene of the accident, and introduced himself as a minister. "Can I be of any assistance?" he asked.

"No, there's nothing you can do," one of last two EMTS at the scene said. He pointed to my tarp-covered vehicle. "He's the only one left and he's dead."

Dick stood in front of the man for several seconds before he said, "I'd like to pray for him."

"There's no one to pray for," the EMT said. "He's dead."

"I know," Dick said, "but I feel I need to pray for him."

"He's dead."

Dick didn't believe in praying for the dead. It was the first time he had even thought of doing such a thing, but he felt a strong, inner compulsion. "I need to pray for him. God told me." Those were words that didn't come naturally from the pastor.

"He's dead. Dead. Besides, it's—it's an ugly sight."

13

"I was a medic in Vietnam," Dick said. "Whatever is under that tarp can't be worse than I've already seen."

I'm thankful that Dick ignored his own theology, which was not to pray for dead people, and instead embraced the will of God. He was obedient. "I must pray for him," Dick insisted.

Perhaps as much to shut him up as anything, the EMT relented and allowed Dick to get into the car and pray for me. He lifted the tarp and crawled in the car through the back window. He saw my condition and put his right hand on my right shoulder and began to pray.

In the meantime, the authorities had identified me and notified the church, my wife, and my three children. They were careful not to tell them I was dead, but only that I had been involved in a collision. The word spread about the accident and within minutes requests to pray for me went out all over the country. By the time Dick had begun to pray for me, thousands of others had already begun to plead to God for my life. It was a prayer chain that went around the country regardless of denomination.

I make a point of this because in the past few years I've met at least two hundred people in various parts of the United States who heard about me that day and prayed for me while I was lying dead on the bridge.

"Someone from our church called and I prayed for you," one man said. "I remember your story and it was very dramatic."

The most powerful testimony came from a man in Illinois. After he heard me speak in church, he came up to me. He was visibly shaking. "This is amazing!" he said. "I walked into our prayer meeting in Indiana, which is where I lived in January of 1989. That night our pastor read a fax from the Baptist General Convention of Texas. He told us about a pastor who had been on his way home from a conference and had been horribly injured in a car wreck."

"That sounds like me," I said.

"We all got on our knees at church that night and prayed for you."

Tears filled my eyes and I hardly knew what to say.

He extended his hand, grabbed mine, and shook it. "You're the man! You're the man! You're the guy we prayed for that night."

"Here I am and the prayers worked. God answers prayer."

I knew nothing of prayers or the reports of my accident. At that very moment, I basked in the joy of heaven.

Dick knelt inside the car and prayed for that horrible, mangled body. He had no idea how long he prayed and that's not important. He prayed: That's what's important. After a period of time, he paused and sang. He prayed again. The second time he paused, he began to sing, "What a Friend We Have in Jesus."

Before he finished the first stanza, I had begun to sing with him. Again I want to point out that I didn't encounter anything typical of an NDE. I was in heaven, filled with utter joy and more alive than I'd ever been before. My next conscious moment I heard my own voice singing with Dick.

Dick said my voice was weak, barely audible, but I sang.

He scooted out from the tarp and yelled, "He's alive! This man is alive!"

The first technician shook his head. "I told you, he's dead," the EMT said.

"I'm sure that's what you want to think," said the other, "but—"

"He's alive!"

No matter what Dick said, he couldn't convince those two men. They had checked me long before Dick came on the scene. "We're professionals," one of them said. "We know a dead man when we see one."

"He's alive! Just come over and let me show you."

The ambulance was ready to move out, but Dick knew that the ambulance was my only hope for survival. Another vehicle stood by to take away my body, but by state law, they had to wait for a county official to come so he could declare me dead before they could transport my body to a mortuary.

Dick begged the men to listen. He yelled. He pleaded. Finally he stood in the middle of the bridge. "I'm going to lie down on this bridge and you'll have to run over me. He's alive and I'm not leaving until you examine him again."

The two men looked at each other. One of them shrugged as if to ask, "What's the harm?"

To humor Dick and to get him off the middle of the bridge, they went to my car and checked my pulse.

"He's alive! He really is alive," one EMT said to the other.

By then, Dick said, I audibly moaned.

The medical technicians leaped into action. They couldn't pull me out of the car so they ordered the Jaws of Life to pry open the crushed vehicle to get me out. They talked to me and encouraged me to hold on.

Once the Jaws of Life freed me, the EMTs placed me in an ambulance and transported me to a clinic. They were unable to do anything for me—I'm not sure they even took me out of the ambulance.

I was conscious enough to feel the pain and begged for medication. They didn't want me to lapse into unconsciousness, so they were under instructions to refuse me medication. They took me to the hospital in Huntsville to do an assessment to determine if there was any hope. The doctors there decided that the only chance of survival would be to transport me to a trauma center. Houston was the closest. I eventually was taken by ambulance because in the inclement weather they were not able to fly helicopters. Helicopters can't fly with low ceilings; the pilots have to be able to see where they're going. So they transported me by ambulance to Memorial Hermann Hospital. I got there at six-fifteen that night following an accident that had happened at eleven-forty-five in the morning.

The bridge over Lake Livingston was built as a memorial. I sometimes think that it's also a memorial to me. Although they no longer use the bridge, it's still there. I have pictures of the bridge and the accident. Most of all, of course, I have the memories.

My decision to drive over that bridge changed my life. I drove onto the bridge as a healthy, thirty-eight-year-old pastor on his way to lead Wednesday night services at his church. I drove on the bridge as a husband and a father of three children. I drove on as the son of Ralph and Billie Piper, and a man with many friends. I was in the prime of life, really, poised for what I hoped would be a life of service to the Lord and a meaningful existence.

I started across inside my own car; I left in the back of an ambulance. I would never again be the same—not physically, emotionally, spiritually, or in any other way.

I had not been particularly afraid of death. In fact, at age thirty-eight I didn't think much about dying. But since that experience, all fears, hesitancies, and questions are gone.

That bridge was the transition between a life with relatively few concerns to one devoted to helping others enjoy a meaningful existence. Even if they experience horrible changes, losses, or tragedies, in the end, they can go to heaven—to the place Jesus prepared for those who follow him. They go there because they've already made their reservations.

Before my disaster on the bridge, I had only a general idea of how much suffering and anguish goes on in lives around me, all through our Western countries, far away from the battlefields, and in the midst of simple daily living. Because I endured so much after my accident, I am more open and aware of what others must face. I have realized that most of us have to endure hardships and difficulties.

In a previous book I recounted some of the amazing stories that have come out because of my accident. I'm certainly not the only person who has suffered, and it helps—and humbles—me to remember that.

For example, a couple from Sweden was vacationing in the South Pacific when the infamous tsunami struck. She had a copy of *90 Minutes in Heaven* in her hand and it was washed out of her hands. For days she didn't know if her husband survived. He did survive, and they found each other. She had been a believer, but he had not. She bought a second copy of *90 Minutes in Heaven* for him. After the ordeal, he read it and became a believer.

I've met Hurricane Katrina victims who have read my two earlier books. Because they know I understand loss and pain, they've eagerly told me their stories. Middle-aged men have walked into work on a Monday morning and by noon they were jobless. One man said his boss called him to his office, and said, "You've been a faithful employee for twenty-three years, and we think you're one of the best performers here. However, because of company consolidation, we have to let you go. We'll give you a nice severance pay."

As the man told me that story, he wiped his eyes and said, "I'm forty-nine years old. What am I going to be able to do now that will replace that job?"

A couple tried for years to have children and finally they succeeded. They had a boy. Two years later, he died from a rare blood disorder. "How can this be?" the wife asked. "Why did God give us a son and take him away after two years?"

After I spoke in Ohio, a highly emotional woman stopped at the book-signing table. "I was at the World Trade Center on 9/11. I know I'll never be the same again. I've desperately tried to find a new way to live since that day. How can anyone be so heartless and cruel to slaughter thousands of innocent people like that?"

I didn't know the answer to such questions then. I still don't know the answer. I do know there is an answer because God cares and promises never to leave us. I also know there is comfort from God even when we don't have answers.

I could tell many stories of loss—and some of them are in other parts of this book. For now, I want to point again to the bridge as a metaphor for our lives. I didn't leap from the bridge, and I didn't anticipate what lay ahead. Like most of us, there was no way for me to anticipate what I would encounter when I crossed that bridge.

I left the bridge different than I had been when I started across. Since that accident, I've had thirty-four major operations, spent thirteen months in the hospital followed by two years of rehabilitation, and lost years of fellowship with my family and friends. I've lost physical abilities I'll never reclaim. I live with constant but manageable pain, and even now I feel a slight but momentary fear whenever a big truck comes toward me, even if it's two lanes away.

I could focus on the things I've lost or the pain I live with, but I've chosen not to do that. Instead I've chosen to remember that years after the accident I was able to walk my daughter down the aisle at her wedding. Just as the wedding march started, Nicole turned toward me and said, "Daddy, I'm glad you're here today."

We both knew what she meant.

Although since January 18, 1989, I have asked many times why God let me live, the years subsequent have brought much joy and more definitive answers.

Since the accident, I've watched all three of my children graduate from college. I've had fifteen years of ministry in cities in Texas such as Alvin, Rosharon, Plano, and Pasadena. I've traveled and spoken steadily since 2004 and been introduced to millions as the Minister of Hope. I've been interviewed for hundreds of radio programs, magazines, and newspapers. I've appeared on NBC's *Today Show, The Coral Ridge Hour* with Dr. D. James Kennedy, *Life Today* with James Robison, and dozens of other TV shows. I've become an evangelist to tell people about answered prayer, new beginnings, and miracles, and most of all, to share with them the reality of heaven.

I am constantly awestruck when I realize how God has used my story. When Cecil Murphey and I sat down to write *90 Minutes in Heaven*, there was no way I could possibly have imagined the way it would impact others. People from Sweden to Korea, from Hawaii to England, and from Norway to Mexico have been encouraged by the story of the dead man talking and walking.

The guy who died on that bridge lives today. Even after thirty-four surgeries and months in the hospital, I still want to encourage everyone to go forward—regardless of the bridges they're forced to cross.

I've thought of a way to help people look at crossing bridges in their lives. One of my friends refers to his life as chapters in a book. He says, "My life is a book, and I'm the protagonist." Using that image, suppose you decided to write your life story. At what point would you begin a section with these words: "A new chapter in my life opened when . . ."?

THREE

Yes, It's Real

"How do you know you were really dead?" skeptics ask. They've read and heard reports of various people who had out-of-body experiences. "How do you know it was real?"

I know it was real because I experienced it. No matter what anyone says or thinks, I know heaven is real. I know in the way that we can only know about a thing by having experienced it.

I'll also say that when I reached heaven, I had a kind of body—and words cannot begin to explain it. I can say only that my body was perfect and there were no scars and I never felt any pain. The earthly shell that was my soul's container lay there under that tarp on that bridge. The real me—the inner me— stood at the gates of heaven in the presence of those who had gone before me.

One more thing I want say about the reality of heaven: There was no transition, no floating, no moving from the bridge upward to heaven. I was alive and driving across the bridge when the truck came at me; the next moment of awareness, I was in heaven.

There was no sense that I had a choice in the matter. My destiny had been decided twenty-two years earlier.

Many of those who speak of NDEs have similar stories. I'm not trying to dispute or argue with them, only to point out that my experience was distinctly different. Many of them report things that are not borne out by what the Bible says. Everything that happened to me in heaven is confirmed by what I had read, and have since read, in the Bible. I found verses in the book of Revelation after my return to earth that describe exactly what I experienced. I had read those verses before, of course, but I hadn't paid much attention to them.

For example, the concept of being gathered together with our loved ones. We read about the streets of gold and the music. I never paid much attention to those verses. Here's one: "[God] will wipe every tear from their eyes. There will be no more death or mourning or crying or pain, for the old order of things has passed away" (Revelation 21:4b†).

I read through those passages and didn't know if they were literal or symbolic. It didn't matter to me on earth. But now that I have been there, I can report, those verses in Revelation refer to literal streets of gold: "The great street of the city was of pure gold, like transparent glass" (Verse 21b).

In 1 Corinthians 15:35–58, the apostle Paul writes about the bodies we will have after we reach heaven. "The body that is sown is perishable, it is raised imperishable . . . it is sown a natural body, it is raised a spiritual body" (Verses 42b–44). Every person I saw in my brief trip to heaven was totally healthy. For example, my grandmother had false teeth, but when I saw her in heaven, her teeth were real. Her body was perfect as it had never been on earth.

After my return and when I was able to read the Bible again, 1 Corinthians 15 and the book of Revelation took on a different meaning for me. I read the words on paper about the music, but inside my head, I could hear the heavenly sounds.

As I read descriptions and statements about heaven, I'd hear myself say, "Yes, absolutely, yes."

When people ask, "How do you know if this was real and how do you know that this really happened to you?"

My answer is simple: "I know it is real because I experienced what the Bible says will happen. Everything that happened to me in heaven confirms what the Bible says. I saw, felt, and experienced heaven." I have no further arguments to make.

That's also the reason I didn't talk about my experience to anyone for at least two years. I was sure they wouldn't believe or they would be skeptical or say it was purely my imagination. It was a holy thing—too holy, too sacred to argue about. Somebody said to me one time, "So you kept this as a sacred secret?"

That's it exactly: a sacred secret. I kept it to myself. I don't think of it as being selfish. God had allowed me to experience heaven. I didn't have any impression or guidance that He wanted me to go around and talk about it.

I began to speak openly about my heavenly experience because my friend David Gentiles felt I should not keep it as a sacred secret. Other people didn't just encourage me—they insisted I needed to share my story. I still hesitated and I prayed a great deal. Finally I went ahead and told the story and I'm still overwhelmed at the response. Sharing my story seems to have made such a profound difference in people's lives.

I also realize that no matter what I say, some people will not believe, accept, or understand. That's all right with me. "The heaven thing is a faith thing," I often say. "No amount of evidence I offer is ever going to convince anybody who isn't inclined to believe. They would have to experience it for themselves."

I can tell people about heaven, a joyously perfect eternity, and about God's grace, but until they experience those things for themselves, they have to grasp them by faith. But one day, I remind them, heaven will become a reality. Grace is not something I can explain; faith is not something that I can impart. I'm not asking that people have faith in me. I can only say, "I truly experienced heaven. I hope you'll be able to believe these things for yourself."

Children often have difficulty in grasping the concept of death because it's usually far removed from their experiences. They don't usually think about their own deaths—and why should they? They're too busy learning about life. However, they are extremely perceptive and they pick up on things. They usually start to grapple with such issues when Grandma passes away. They feel a sense of loss even if they can't understand all the implications of death and heaven.

When I talk in churches about dying, most of the children have some small concept of it. They like to talk to me afterward and I can tell that they're fascinated by the fact that I have died and yet I'm able to be present and talk to them. To my surprise, they want to talk about death and, unlike many adults, they're not afraid of the topic.

Kids constantly e-mail and write me letters. For instance, Lucas, a ten-year-old boy from Arizona, wrote me. He wanted to know more about heaven and what will happen when he dies. I answered Lucas the best I could. Although his questions had to do with a school project, I hope that one day my words will impact him as he faces serious loss or moves toward his own demise.

Here's something that has amazed me: Between 10 and 15 percent of the people who come through a book-signing line are fifteen years old or younger. They're not there to buy the book for Grandma; they want it for themselves. Some have turned my story into projects such as book reports or science papers.

Occasionally I speak at youth groups where the average age is thirteen or fourteen. When I speak to adults, I usually talk about seeing my grandfather—he was the first person I saw when I reached heaven. When I speak to kids, I focus on Mike Wood, the young man who was a good friend and had a tremendous spiritual impact on me as a kid.

Mike was a member of the Sunday school class I joined at age sixteen, and he became a special friend. Mike was completely faithful, utterly reliable, and I admired him for his unequivocal dedication to being a Christian. He was a big kid and a star athlete. That guy had everything in the world going for him and yet, in his humility, he knew he needed Jesus and focused his life on following the Lord. Mike's death in an accident devastated me. That's the first time death had a truly strong, personal meaning for me. I never forgot him. When I saw him again in heaven, Mike was happy and filled with joy just to be there. The reunion was spectacular.

Even though it's hard to explain to kids what death is, one way I've found helpful is to compare it with *The Wizard of Oz*. Almost every child knows that story or has seen the film on TV. When the house falls on the Wicked Witch of the East, she is dead.

Children remember that scene and they understand that the

Wicked Witch ceased to exist from that time on. I explain then that, after my accident, as far as people on earth were concerned, I ceased to exist—at least for ninety minutes. I try to point out that the apostle Paul often contrasted being present in the body to mean he was absent from heaven. At one time he wrote, "For to me, living means living for Christ, and dying is even better" (Philippians 1:21**). He is either alive doing the Lord's work or he is with Christ in heaven. Children can identify with that even if in the larger scheme they don't understand the consequences of death. They know that when people die, they don't get to stay here on earth.

Children are not as afraid of dying because they don't understand death, especially the finality of it. Older folks understand and they want to discover what they need to do to prepare for it. Children want to know about heaven, but they'd rather hear about Jesus. They'd rather hear about the loving Savior and the one who calls children to himself. This reality, the reality of Jesus, is just as important, if not more so, for if they understand Jesus and accept him, they will have everything they need for full lives now and heaven as a reward at the end.

Perhaps the most difficult thing that happens when people have overpowering changes in their lives is they find it difficult to accept the reality of the event. They remember how life used to be and they want to go back to the former way. They can't accept that their lives have changed.

To observers that often seems strange.

"Don't they know things are not the way they used to be? Can't they see the difference?" Yes, they can. But to "see" the difference and to "admit" the difference may be far apart.

Some things happen to us that irrevocably change us in spite of anything we can do. Things are different after that point than they ever were before.

Sometimes I ask people to close their eyes. Then I tell them, "Remember the worst thing or the biggest tragedy of your life. What's the worst thing?"

I get a variety of answers because everyone has things that have happened that they consider terrible and everyone has had things that change them irrevocably.

Then I ask, "What are you doing about coping with the worst things? What are you doing now to deal with your new reality?"

A woman from San Antonio told me a horrendous story. One day a man burst into her office with a gun and opened fire. He killed two people. He shot her in the face and left her for dead.

She phoned me to say, "I read your book and I wanted to thank you for redirecting me." She referred to the changes and decisions I made after my return to earth. "Thank you for getting me off of what I was going to do about my face. I have to accept the fact that it's not going to be the same. It isn't. But I can take the experience that I've been through, which is not like many other people's, and try to help others who have gone through painful and traumatic things in their lives. Thank you for being courageous and for showing me the way."

That woman's story and others I hear encourage me to talk about my experience. As they listen, hope grows inside them. They sense there is more than the problems they now face.

Heaven is real. I don't have the slightest doubt. That's why I can encourage others—no matter how awful their situation—and remind them that this is preparation for the glorious life ahead.

FOUR

The Results of Decisions

We rarely realize the seriousness of most of our decisions. I'm not just talking about the immense choices such as career change or getting married. We make choices—big and small—every day, and in making those simple choices, we rarely realize how different life will become. Dancer and choreographer Agnes de Mille said it well in these words: "No trumpets sound when the important decisions of our life are made. Destiny is made known silently."

And every choice we make changes our lives in some way. Few of us pause to reflect on the changes in our lives. Sure, we have some sense of change when things go terribly wrong for us—such as being let go at our job or facing a divorce we don't want. But when we look closely at our lives, most of us will discover that the apparently minor decisions have major impacts. My decision to turn right at Trinity Pines is an example.

We make choices every day and most of them seem insignificant and minor. And they may be. But most of the time, we have no way to know which of those simple decisions will alter our lives. There was no way I could have known that an eighteen-wheeler would crash into my Ford at 11:45 that morning as I was about to exit that bridge. Hundreds of times over the years, I've thought of how life would have been different if I had made a different decision and taken the other path home.

Isn't that the way most of us function? We look back and ask, "What if I had . . . ?" "If I had only . . ." We also know that we can't undo those choices. We need to be mindful that every choice has consequences. It's as simple as choosing which seat to take on a bus or which flight to take to reach a destination. Years ago, a friend had reservations on a flight from New Delhi to Bangalore. He stayed with friends, and when they went to leave for the airport, the friend's car wouldn't start. By the time they reached the airport, they'd missed the flight by ten minutes. That plane crashed shortly after takeoff and everyone on board died.

We never know about those decisions—sometimes it's our own choices, sometimes God intervenes, and at other times they are the unexplainables of life.

The long-term consequences of our decision can take years to reveal themselves.

Who would have dreamed of the results that would follow my simple decision about which road to take home? Years after the accident, I wrote about the experience, and I've been interviewed about it hundreds of times. My book has been translated into several languages. And my story is changing innumerable lives. People have chosen to read my book or listen to the radio interviews, and sometimes that decision to read or listen has changed lives.

I've received countless phone calls from radio stations after my interview, telling me of the impact the show had on their listeners.

I remember one station manager who called and said, "I wanted you to know that we've had three phone calls—people who actually made confessions of faith directly because of your testimony."

Every day I receive hundreds of e-mails from people wanting to let me know they were personally transformed and gave themselves to Christ after hearing about my time in heaven.

Who would have believed that I could tell my story and that lives would be eternally different? I could never have predicted that people would make life-changing decisions based on listening to me share my experiences.

Others come to me and tell me their strange or unusual stories. Since my first book came out, people have come up to me at churches or bookstores and they want to talk about their near-death experiences. They ask if they can talk to me privately.

"If you'll wait until I've finished here," I tell them.

Once we get alone, they tell me about their near-death experiences. Such stories have received a lot of publicity during the past thirty years. Most of them tell of a dark tunnel, a bright glowing light, and then seeing loved ones beckoning to them before they suddenly return to their bodies. I don't judge these accounts. Who am I to judge if they are true or not? I merely listen and share my story and what it says in the Bible.

But a few of those who talk to me have a difference experience.

"I smelled sulfur. I saw demons. I heard people scream in torment." Those three statements are typical and they nearly always add, "That experience terrified me. I was overwhelmed by fear." They had such horrible moments that they can't shake the memories—even years later. Often the hellishness of that near-death experience is enough to bring them to God.

Such encounters change lives. As terrifying as their stories are, I tell them that it's God's grace to show them what life will be like in eternity without Jesus Christ.

"I had an experience," I tell them, "but I died and immediately went to heaven."

"How can I be sure that's where I'll go?" I'm always delighted for the opportunity to explain.

What I want to emphasize in this chapter is that life is about decisions—and especially about making the right ones. My decision at sixteen determined what happened to me at thirty-eight.

When I spoke at a rural Texas church, I said, "You may not think this is important, but you decided to put your clothes on and come this morning to be inside God's house. It's altogether possible that this is a rendezvous with destiny. Right here. Today. Attending church may be something you do every Sunday or you may have come to hear a dead man talk. I don't know why you came this morning, but you made a decision to attend. This decision could affect the rest of your life.

"God forbid that you would get hit by a big truck on your way, but you might. After all, I was on my way to church when I got hit. I had even prepared my message for the service that Wednesday night. But if that were to happen to you today, where would you go?

"We all know there's no immunity from death. Whether it happens when we're sixteen, thirty-eight, or seventy-eight, we're all going to die. The decisions you make today can affect where you go when the time comes."

Decisions. Decisions. At the time we make them, most seem innocuous, incidental, or minor. And most of them are. But you never know when you're going to make a decision that will change your life completely.

FIVE

Why Doesn't God Want Me to Be Happy?

The woman burst into tears before she asked me, "Why doesn't God want me to be happy?" Before I could respond she gave me a long series of things wrong with her life.

"I just want to be happy in this life. I pray for God to make me happy, but he never does."

She hurried away soon after that, but I wanted to ask, "Don't you think you have some responsibility for your misery?"

Her question implied that God is a taskmaster and enjoys our misery. It's a subtle accusation that he can't stand it when we're doing well so he disrupts our lives to make us miserable. That's totally erroneous.

One of the things the Bible makes clear is that God wants us to be happy. He created us to be happy. The problem is that *we* allow things into our lives that don't make us personally contented or joyful. We make bad choices. We choose things that will bring us temporary pleasure but in the long run harm us.

For example, years ago I spoke with a recovering alcoholic. He said he began to drink because he thought all his friends had more fun than he did and they enjoyed life. So he tried a few drinks. "And it was fun. During the first party I attended everything was funny. Hilarious." The alcohol loosened him up and he got rid of his inhibitions. Before long, however, the alcohol took over his life. He said, "I had my first drink at twenty and for the next fifteen years I was never sober."

He found a kind of happiness, but it was an illusion. From far away, partying seemed exciting and attractive, but the happy life his friends seemed to have was only a façade. That's not what God offers us. He wants us to have a good life—a meaningful life on earth—so that when we experience the reality of heaven, it truly is like crossing a bridge. We go from a good life to a perfect life.

Heaven is about eternity, and it's eternal life then, but God is interested in our having abundant life now. Jesus said it this way: ". . . I have come that they may have life, and have it to the full" (John 10:10b†). The apostle Peter wrote, "Though you have not seen [Jesus], you love him; and even though you do not see him now, you believe in him and are filled with inexpressible and glorious joy" (1 Peter 1:8).

I believe that deep, inner joy is the surest sign of the purpose of God at home in a human being. As Bruce Larson once said, grimness isn't a Christian virtue. There aren't any continuously sad saints. If God is the center of our lives, joy is inevitable. If we have no joy we miss the heart of the good news, and our bodies as well as our souls will suffer the consequences.

Sometimes I think of the children's song that begins, "I've got the joy, joy, joy down in my heart." That's the idea. It doesn't mean going around with a goofy grin or the attitude that nothing is ever wrong. It means having a joyful heart. Even if circumstances are difficult, painful, or sad, we can still have joy within us.

I have two favorite examples of the divine joy in action. One is an account that appears in Acts 16:16–34. Paul and Silas were attacked by a crowd in the city of Philippi: ". . . and the magistrates ordered them to be stripped and beaten. After they had been severely flogged, they were thrown into prison, and the jailer was commanded to guard them carefully. Upon receiving such orders, he put them in the inner cell and fastened their feet in the stocks" (Verses 22–24†).

The flogging would have been severe. So how did those two men react? "About midnight Paul and Silas were praying and singing hymns to God, and the other prisoners were listening to them" (Verse 25).

They must have been in severe pain. Yet despite their pain and even though they were in prison, those two men prayed. They praised God. In short, they expressed their joy in Jesus Christ. They were able to endure the pain because of something deep inside them: the knowledge of their relationship with the Lord. And the other prisoners were listening to them. These were hardened criminals, and yet the absolute joy that Silas and Paul expressed made the criminals take notice—it obviously touched them.

The second story is recorded in Acts 5. The previous chapter in Acts tells about Peter and John's arrest. They spent the night in jail and the Jewish leaders had them released the next day, but first, they commanded them not to preach about Jesus. The two apostles said, "Judge for yourselves whether it is right in God's sight to obey you rather than God" (Acts 4:19). They were brought before the

Jewish leaders a second time and again told to stop their public preaching about Jesus. This time, "They called in the apostles and had them flogged. Then they ordered them never again to speak in the name of Jesus, and they let them go" (5:40**).

Here's the response: "The apostles left the high council rejoicing that God had counted them worthy to suffer disgrace for the name of Jesus" (Verse 41). The next verse goes on to speak of their activities of going to the temple and into homes to teach and to preach the gospel. Their joy was so contagious, the Jewish leaders were afraid of them and the people embraced them.

Those Christians had powerful spiritual motivation. And you know what that was? They knew that the Holy Spirit was with them, and they knew they were doing the right thing. They knew that nothing could happen to them outside of God's control. What could be a higher motivation than that?

Someone once said, "Christians are the laughing cavaliers of Christ." I believe joy is an *inevitable* part of the Christian walk. When God is with you, how can you be anything but joyful? A gloomy Christian is a contradiction.

Yet, I go to churches where gracious individuals invite me, and when I stare down from the pulpit, I'm amazed at the faces that look as if they've just had a long swig of dill pickle juice. I've been to some churches where I've felt like saying, "I could hang meat in the building and it would be perfectly preserved because of the frosty lack of fellowship." The people come but they lack the warmth and spirit that attracts others. If only they realized the abundance the Lord offers them, they couldn't help but have a smile on their faces.

A couple of years ago I preached in a warm, exciting church and the people responded. I saw joy and happiness etched in many faces. The pastor asked if I could spend time with a family from the congregation. "Of course," I said.

After the service, I went into the pastor's study. An older couple came in right behind me, and the husband pushed a wheelchair. The man in the wheelchair was obviously their son. I assumed he had cerebral palsy.

After they introduced themselves and their son, we talked for several minutes before the father said, "Our son tried to kill himself. He was miserable and depressed about his life. Several years ago, he shot himself in the head."

As I stared at the son, I judged his age to be about thirty. All these years you've been in a wheelchair, I thought, because of a terrible tragic mistake you made.

The young man's mental faculties hadn't been affected, although he wasn't very verbal. As I listened, the parents' attitude surprised me. They weren't the least bit ashamed or bitter. I admired them for the sincere, inner joy that shone through their eyes.

Finally the father said, "Our son has a question. He was miserable for years, but now he is able to see life differently. Even in this condition, he knows life is worth living. Consequently he wants to know how he can take his circumstances and *intentionally* help somebody else."

The question shocked me but I realized that the son had moved beyond remorse or shame and wanted his life to count for something. His words came out slowly, with pauses between each one, but one thing he said struck me as powerful: "I want to stop others from attempting suicide like I did."

We talked for quite a while and I made several suggestions, but my first and most important one was this: "You need to chronicle your story. Put in writing what happened to you. Your story might never get into print, but you need perspective on what happened to you. What led up to the attempt to take your life? Why were you so unhappy? What has happened to you since? When you go back over it, you may actually discover dimensions of it that you never really thought about, so do that. Can you do that?"

He smiled, nodded, and said, "Yes, yes, I can do that."

"After you've done that, find people that you trust and share the story with them. Listen to their response."

Before he could object, I added, "You'll be amazed. You'll have people say to you, 'I know someone who is going through a very similar situation as you did,' or 'They have a kid about the same age as you were when this happened and they're afraid for the child.' You'll be surprised how your testimony can touch others."

His eyes brightened and he smiled. He knew he had found an outlet for service.

"Just think of it this way," I said. "Your story could save someone else from doing the same thing that you did."

"Do you really think I could—?"

I saw doubt in his eyes so I asked, "What if you wrote your story and it saved a life? Or perhaps many lives?"

"Yes. Yes. I think I'll do that."

"I think you should. You may need some professional help with it but that's okay. First do it in your own words. Then based on the response you get and the suggestions on writing it better, you can consider sharing the story in a public form, to whatever extent that you're comfortable. Maybe your parents will help you. Maybe they can tell their side of the story as well. But part of the process of getting through this catharsis is to relive it and move past the experience so you can make a difference by showing others how to be happy and to enjoy their lives."

He thanked me several times and so did his parents.

The last I heard, the elderly parents still cared for the son at home. He also has some kind of part-time job where he makes a small amount of money. Whatever free time he had, the young man worked on writing his story. "He's determined to finish it and help others," his mother wrote me.

Part of the reason I share this story is because of the parents. Whatever dreams they had for their son's life and his future are gone forever. But even in the midst of that, they exuded a quiet joy and inner peace. My assumption is that in the years since their son's attempt on his own life, they had fought the battles of disappointment and despair and had come to rely on spiritual resources they might never have realized.

That older couple—individuals most of us might feel sorry for—could teach many believers what joy is like. Joy isn't an absence of problems or having nothing hard in life. They proved that. Joy—true inner, godly joy—is the result of knowing the circumstances and still being able to say, "It is well with my soul."

Here's another example. A man talked to an older woman about her invalid husband, who has a number of serious physical ailments. "He never has a day without pain," the wife said.

"I'm sorry, really, for what you're going through," the man said.

"Thank you and I know you mean well," she said, "but we have had sixty wonderful years together. We have been happy and we've raised two wonderful sons. Despite problems and especially now, life has been so good for us and God has blessed us far more than we ever deserve. He's sick and both of us know he won't live much longer, but we've been happy together. We still have peace and joy in our heart for those happy years. Why shouldn't we rejoice and give thanks to God?"

She went on to quote the words of Job after Satan attacked his life: "Should we accept only good things from the hand of God and never anything bad?" (Job 2:10b**).

That's joy at work. That's spiritual happiness.

My questions to unhappy people are here. What would enable some people to be joyful for what they have and not to be bitter over what went wrong or what they don't have? Paul and Silas proved it. Peter and the other apostles lived it. If they showed that such a life is possible, what do *you* need to do to be happy? What do *you* need to do to discover the inner peace God wants to give you?

Karen Altom e-mailed me a story that I want to share. She's from Huntsville, Texas, about twelve miles from where I had my accident. "I was involved in an auto accident just west of town. I grew up the daughter of a minister and have always had a strong faith, and I could tell you ways that I have seen God work since the moment the accident occurred. I suffered a broken leg. My five-year-old son was with me and uninjured, thanks be only to God. He sat directly behind the driver's seat, asleep, with his head against the window, and in the photo of the car anyone can see that area was untouched.

"After a Life Flight to Memorial Hermann hospital in Houston, I remember thinking that I would be okay in about two or three months because I had *only* a broken leg. I had a shattered femur and, as you well know, that demands a long recovery.

"I related to much of what you wrote in your first book. Thankfully I haven't had to have the external fixation [pins screwed into the bone and secured outside the skin with clamps and rods to immobilize the bone and allowed a fracture to heal]. But while I read your book, I cried barrels of tears and prayed fervently that I never would have to have one. I am finally walking and am now having shoes made to 'level me out.' I look forward to the day that I can take a walk around the block in my new 'tennies.' That should be sometime in the next couple of weeks.

"Thank you for sharing your story. I appreciate the description of heaven and my anticipation and longing for home is now even greater.

"I also must tell you that I appreciate it from another perspective. I have done my best during these past four years to find the blessings in every day and look for the things for which I am thankful. Things like talking to my children at eye level rather than looking down at them while I sat in a wheelchair for months. I like that. I think of other things such as eating comfort food and having a real reason on which to blame the weight gain (although the getting it off is not so fun right now!). And, truthfully, reading your book and thanking God that at least mine wasn't that bad! I'm sorry for the pain you've gone through but I do know that all things work together for good to them that love God."

She said she looked for things to give thanks for. That's the evidence of the happiness and inner joy Karen has found. She's not bitter and not complaining. She accepts it and moves on.

I've thought a great deal about the question the woman asked that I reported at the beginning of this chapter: "Why doesn't

God want me to be happy?" I've pointed out several passages from the Bible that make it clear God wants us to be happy. I've given two biblical accounts and shared a couple of stories of people who have found joy in the midst of their hardships.

I wish I had a chance to meet that woman again. I'd have a question for her: Why don't you want to be happy?

I think that's the real question.

Standing Alone

In my travels across the world since 2004, I've heard many remarkable stories and some of them have brought tears to my eyes. I can say without doubt that the story that touched me most deeply occurred in Lyngdal, Norway.

On a trip to Norway in July of 2006, I received an invitation to preach in a small church in a western town named Lyngdal. The building probably couldn't have held more than 250 people. That night the attendance was almost double the capacity. People filled the balcony (which no one ever used), others sat in the side room and looked through windows, and visitors stood in any spot that wasn't already filled.

That evening I spoke about my trip to heaven and about God answering prayers. At the request of the pastor, at the end of the service, I extended an invitation (or altar call) in which I invited people to come forward for prayer and counseling if they wanted to become Christians and follow Jesus Christ. Many people came forward for prayer.

That in itself wasn't unusual. In all the churches in Norway and Sweden when I gave invitations, I've had excellent responses, but one thing stands out about that evening.

I spotted a young man, seventeen years old, and later learned his name was Billal. Two young women about his age came forward with him. Both of them looked like stereotypical Scandinavians— blond and blue-eyed. But Billal wasn't like anyone else present. Although extremely handsome, with black hair and black eyes, I assumed he was Middle Eastern. As I learned a few minutes later, that was correct.

Although Billal's family had come from a Muslim country, they had immigrated to Germany and later to Sweden. His family was Muslim and they had raised him in that faith. I don't know the details, but only a few days before I arrived, Billal had left Islam and turned to Jesus Christ as his Savior. That caused a great celebration among his friends and especially those two girls who knelt beside him.

It was also a time of great remorse. When Billal told his parents of his conversion, they were absolutely irate. They pleaded with him to return to Islam, threatened him if he didn't, and when he remained resolute, they threw him out of the house. "You may never return," they told him. "To us, you are dead." The boy's father threatened to put out a contract for his death.

Billal loved his family and wanted peace with them, but he loved Jesus Christ more. He refused to recant and never tried to return home, but he still loved his family and felt especially remorseful over the separation from his younger brother. He came to the family of the two girls with only the clothes he wore. He had no food and no money. They were Christians who had helped him find his way to God so they lovingly took him into their house so he could live there and finish his secondary education.

Billal came to the service and his heart was sad and he was also afraid for his life. He knew his father could be brutal and might follow through and have him murdered. The young man cried as he knelt at the front of the church. Another minister went over and prayed with him. After a few minutes, the minister asked me if I could come and join them. I went over to talk to him and he told me his story.

Most young people in Scandinavia speak fluent English so we needed no translators. "I have come for prayer," he said.

Billal wanted affirmation that he had done the right thing in becoming a Christian. "I love God," he said, but he also needed the assurance that God would take care of him, even if his earthly father decided to kill him.

I assured Billal that God was with him. "Nothing will happen that God will not allow."

The boy was so distraught he could hardly speak. It took a long time for him to tell his story because he could speak only a few sentences between sobs. He remained highly emotional and nothing seemed to encourage him. Several of us settled in around him. I wanted to hear the entire story but even more, I wanted to offer him whatever comfort I could.

We prayed with Billal, and as we did, I thought of a young Muslim man in the States who had gone through a similar experience. After he became a believer, his father had also threatened to kill him. Although he was now in his thirties, his conversion experience had taken place when he was about the same age as that young man. I thought that if Billal could connect with someone who had a similar background, it would help him. Amazingly, although the American young man also had his life threatened, God has not only sustained him through the years, but all of his family eventually became Christians. I told Billal this story and made a mental note to put him in touch with his American counterpart.

I also commended the Norwegian family who had taken him in. "I've met them and I know they won't abandon you. And most of all, Jesus has promised that he is always with you." I quoted a couple of Bible verses and he listened. Sometimes it was a nod, sometimes he said a few words, but mostly he cried.

We prayed and he began to sob again. I prayed for him, for his friends, and for his family. I also asked that God would use his decision to powerfully affect others.

I stood behind the young man and wrapped my arm around him while we prayed. His thin body heaved and the sobs became convulsive. He finally stopped and looked up. He had the most beautiful ink-black eyes I had ever seen.

Just then, I noticed a pool of water on the floor just in front of Billal—a kind of circular pattern that must have been at least nine inches in diameter. I glanced at the ceiling and thought, There must be a leak in the ceiling or else something is wrong with the air conditioning.

Suddenly I realized that they don't have air conditioning in Norway—at least not in any place I'd been. It wasn't raining outside, so I assumed someone must have spilled something on the tile floor. I know it sounds silly to be distracted by something like that, but it was a large puddle of water. My gaze traced it to Billal's feet. The front of his clothes was soaked. The water was his tears. I've been in the ministry a lot of years, but I have never seen anyone shed more tears than that young man. But as they fell from his eyes, they changed from tears of fear to tears of hope.

Since my trip to Norway, I've thought many times of his tears. When someone cries like that, it comes from powerful, deep emotions that can't be faked. Seventeen-year-old boys don't usually cry in public, but it was a heartbreaking situation. This kid was so emotionally shattered, he lost all modesty or fear of ridicule.

As I've reflected on that incident, I can't forget it and I don't want to forget. It reminds me how clearly God understands our tears. The boy was surrounded by loving friends, but even more he was surrounded by God's amazing love.

This incident helps me better to understand that some of the decisions we make will cost us dearly. In Billal's case, it cost him his family. I pray often for the uniting of that family, not only physically but spiritually as well.

Some decisions change our lives radically. Most of us have no idea how seriously those choices will change us, but they do.

That night I was reminded of how difficult it can be to cross over from one way of life to another and as I close my eyes those tears will always be a symbol of that cost. The tears of a seventeen-year-old boy on the threshold not only of manhood but his entire life.

It's sad that Billal must stand alone—or at least he will feel alone most of the time despite the Christians around him. As I ponder that, I think again of the apostle Paul.

In his final letter to Timothy, which Paul apparently wrote only a short time before his death, there are no tears and no remorse. He had walked with the Lord for at least thirty years and he was ready to cross the final bridge. But in this letter he wrote about his trial.

If I have understood correctly, Roman trials began with preliminary questions for them to determine the precise charges against the prisoner. When they brought Paul before the judge for that opening examination, not one of his friends showed up to defend him. In their defense, I want to point out that it would have been dangerous for anyone to stand up and proclaim, "I'm a friend of the accused," when the man was on trial for his life.

I'm sure Paul understood, but just to understand doesn't mean we don't feel hurt or rejected. He wrote, "The first time I was brought before the judge, no one was with me. Everyone had abandoned me. May it not be counted against them. But the Lord stood with me and gave me strength so that I might preach the Good News. . . ." (2 Timothy 4:16–17**).

Sometimes we stand alone because we choose to do that. But sometimes, as in the case of Billal, we stand alone because no one wants to stand with us. I meet a number of people who have to stand alone because they have been abandoned or they have messed up their own lives. Sometimes people come to my meetings or write to tell me that they've made terrible decisions and alienated family and friends, and they ask for prayer to get straightened out. "I want to go to heaven," one woman wrote, "and I know God has a place for me, but I made so many mistakes along the way that I feel as if I'm standing totally alone."

I wish I could say to everyone, "You are not alone. Even if there is no one else with you, Jesus Christ promises, 'Be sure of this: I am with you always, even to the end of the age'" (Matthew 28:20b**).

I also think of another passage from the Bible that often provides comfort for people. In the Old Testament, when the Israelites had conquered most of their enemies, Joshua, their longtime leader, was 110 years old and ready to die. He challenged them to follow

God and added, "Now fear the Lord and serve him with all faithfulness. . . . But if serving the Lord seems undesirable to you, then choose for yourselves this day whom you will serve. . . . But as for me and my household, we will serve the Lord" (Joshua 24:14–15[†]). We need to remember that we never have to stand alone. We make choices and we can always choose for Jesus to clasp our hand and walk with us until we cross the final bridge to heaven.

SEVEN

Hidden Scars

I've gone to places to speak where the leaders have already read my books, which is the reason they invited me. I fly in and rent an SUV at the airport because of the difficulty I have getting in and out of smaller cars.

Many times I've pulled up and seen one or two people at the curb with a wheelchair. When I first began to travel, I didn't pay much attention to such incidents. After a number of such occurrences, I realized they waited for me. They assumed I was sufficiently debilitated that when I got there they'd have to help me into the building.

On several occasions, I've parked my SUV, gotten out, and walked over to the people with the wheelchair. "Hello. Who are you waiting for?"

"We're waiting for the man who's going to speak tonight, Don Piper. He'll pull up here and we'll put him in the wheelchair and take him inside."

"What's the matter with him?"

"Oh, he was in a bad wreck. He's badly injured."

"Really? Well, he must not be very good if he's this bad off. Is he worth listening to?" I have to confess I enjoy the teasing.

"No, he's going to be great." They'll talk about one of my books or perhaps someone has heard my CDs. They'll start to tell me the story of my trip to heaven and back.

Finally I can't hold back. "I'm Don Piper."

"No, you can't be—"

"No, I am. And what's more, I've been Don Piper all my life."

We laugh and the person with the wheelchair usually says, "You look great." If there are two waiting they have a nice little dialogue about how good I look.

"We thought you'd be all scarred—"

"All the scars are hidden," I say. "It's amazing what clothes will do about things like that." Sometimes I stay in my playful mood and tell them I looked like Robert Redford before the plastic surgery.

We have a few minutes of fun, and I say, "You know, if five hundred years from now, any archaeologists should find my remains, they'll announce they've found the missing link. My anatomy has been completely rearranged. I have bone grafts taken from one place and put in a different spot. It's the same story with skin grafts." I truthfully tell them that the X-rays don't make me look like any other human being. "And can you imagine the fun I have going through security at airports?"

When those conversations take place, they're vivid reminders that I'm not the same person I was before my accident. I try to live with it as best I can.

If people don't look too closely at the way I walk, I can fit their concept of normalcy. But because one leg is shorter than the other, even with a built-up shoe I still have a limp. That's a minor issue.

More significant, however, is that I have scars all over my body. Because they're not on my face, most people don't notice. On the outside I'm like everyone else. But peel off my clothes and the scars are evident everywhere. I can't even wear short-sleeved shirts in public without showing horrible scars. This isn't to whine or to say "poor me." I'm thankful for being as healthy as I am. There are things I can't do, but I'm grateful for what I can do. In my worst moments, I think about what I missed in playing with my children during the three to four year recovery. I miss the camping trips we never took, the baseball games we never played, the concerts we never attended, and the sexual intimacy with my wife, Eva, that was impossible. But I am alive and I am able to do most things a middle-aged man can do. And I'm grateful for every step I'm able to take.

I have recovered, but the scars remain. For example, in the summer of 2006, a large crowd of children and teens gathered around me in the lobby after the worship service in Sweden. I never counted, but I think there must have been at least a hundred. For a hundred young people to be present is amazing because less than 2 percent of the Swedish population belong to a church. I was honored that they would want to talk to me and ask me questions.

On that particular day, the kids surrounded me and asked questions—the kind only kids ask, from "How old are you?" to "Will my cat go to heaven?"

Eventually one of them asked, "Can we see your scars?"

I don't mind them seeing the scars, but the only one I can show anybody is on my left arm where I had skin grafts and stitches. My arm works, but it's a gruesome looking scar. So I take off my jacket and roll up my sleeve.

Some will gasp. A few of them will want to touch the scar and that's all right, too. That's how kids are and I don't mind. I believe that's a factor in their learning to accept what really happened to me. I talk about my scars from the platform but now they see them.

Every day when I'm in the shower, I look at these ugly scars. They're better than they were in the beginning, but they will never completely disappear.

But I want people to get beyond the visible scars. I have them and they won't go away. More important are my invisible scars— hidden scars that no one will ever see. But the hidden scars are just as real.

I want people to know that even though I believe in a new normal and that I preach it every chance I can and try to live it, the memories remain. There are all kinds of memories that stay with us: special moments with our lost loved ones; the jobs we used to have and the people with whom we worked; the things we used to own but we've lost; the destructive things we did to ourselves and to others.

God heals us. God forgives us and we hope we can forgive ourselves for all the mistakes we made. Regardless, the scars remain—the hidden scars that remind us of our past.

Even with those hidden scars, we know we can't go back to the nice way things used to be. The past is history. But the old patterns of behavior, the former relationships, and the ways of thinking change slowly. Our past never evaporates. However, it can become less powerful. Life doesn't work like flipping a switch and instantly leaving the darkness for brilliant light—that is, until the moment we cross that final bridge and enter heaven.

I tell people: Be prepared. Don't be shocked by the fact that we never quite erase the memories of the past. Having the hidden scars doesn't mean we won't get over the past, but they do remind us of what once was. It's not bad to reflect on how life used to be and how it is today. The important thing to remember is that no matter how bad things are or were in the past, our future can be better.

Hidden scars can be painful. I'm talking about those deep, inner pains that no one can see from the outside—those feelings of being rejected, unloved, and pushed away. I think of the man who had a series of affairs and said finally, "I never felt loved. I went from one woman to another because I wanted to feel loved. Each time I met a new woman, I tried to convince myself that she was the one." He shook his head slowly. "But she never was."

Or I think of a pilot I met in the hospital. His plane crashed and he was the only survivor. Not only did he have many, many physical pains but he talked briefly about what we often call survivor guilt.

On national television, a young man spoke of his being rescued from a coal mine. He was the only one in the group who survived. He couldn't get beyond that.

A film came out in late 2006 called *Flags of Our Fathers*, about the six men who raised the flag at Iwo Jima on February 23, 1945. None of the survivors felt like heroes. One of them, Ira

Hayes, a Pima Indian, returned to the reservation but apparently he felt guilty because he was considered a hero although so many had sacrificed more. He had more than fifty arrests for drunkenness and died at age 32.

I don't know what anyone could have done for Hayes, but in retrospect, I realize that he carried those invisible scars—scars so deep that he couldn't talk about them. I meet people like him every day.

Many of us learn to live with physical scars and disfigurement, but not everyone can live comfortably with the invisible ones. One way to deal with them is to talk about them. I feel truly honored when people reveal those hidden scars.

People sometimes wait for the crowd to leave after I've spoken and signed books. Even if no one else is around they tend to speak softly. "Can we talk?" they'll ask, or they'll say, "I want to tell you something I've never shared with anyone." After I give them permission, they reveal their hidden scars.

They almost always end up in tears and say, "I've never been able to talk about this before."

It's as if they feel the need to apologize to me, but I try to make them understand, I am blessed that they would trust me enough to show those hidden scars. And I believe that for some people just talking to me—or e-mailing or phoning me—becomes their first major step toward healing those invisible scars.

Today I'm often introduced as the Minister of Hope and that has a nice sound to it, but I want it to be more than some tagline. I want that ministry of hope to say, "I'm here to tell you that God knows every secret scar and loves you. Nothing is too ugly for God."

I want to see people freed from their inner pain. I can assure them that heaven is a place of total tranquillity and perfection. They'll have no scars of any kind there. Jesus will be the only one in heaven to have scars—to remind us how we got there. But I don't want them to wait until they cross that final bridge. I want them to experience healing now.

EIGHT

Get Over It!

In some ways, the statement, "Get over it!" is cruel and unfeeling. It may be said with a smile, but it seems insensitive to me. Somehow it implies that people want to hold on to their pain and grief and someone has to verbally slap them so they move on with their lives. Perhaps some people hang on to their pain and love the attention they receive, but most people I've met struggle to be free of their torment and heartache and pray fervently for their release.

Although I'm put off by the phrase "Get over it!" I have to admit there's also something right about those three words. If we're going to make the best of life, we have to get past the event that brought us the pain and grow from it. Getting past doesn't mean forgetting or never thinking about what happened. Moving beyond means we remember the events and we build on them. The trauma becomes part of the foundation that gives us the courage to move forward.

Jonathan Head from Kernersville, North Carolina, shared his story with me: "I'm not sure where to start this e-mail other than to say your book has been an incredible source of relief and confirmation for my wife and me. One of my wife's coworkers gave her the book last week along with a comment along the lines of I don't know if you can read this but it might help. This is probably the fifth or sixth book that someone has given us over the past three years. I was hesitant to start reading yours but I started over the weekend and finished it last night. Here is why I was hesitant.

"On October 1, 2003, my wife, Glenda, had the worst experience a mother can have. She found our fourteen-year-old son facedown on his bedroom floor. He had died during the night of a heart virus that no one knew he had. Basically his heart stopped beating. She screamed for my help and I can vividly remember her pleas and prayers to God to save her son and put life into him.

"I attempted CPR but to no avail. When the EMTs arrived they said nothing could have been done.

"The news of Eric's death ran through the schools and community very fast, and for the next three days there was a constant stream of visitors at our home. Approximately twelve hundred people attended his memorial service.

"Glenda and I have never doubted that Eric is in heaven, as we knew his salvation experience and his Christian walk. We have learned many things since his death, especially that his witness was even more than we knew about. His death has been the topic of more than one high school English paper written by his friends describing the impact he had on their lives.

"I saw a number of similarities in your book to our experiences over the past three years. We receive comments on a pretty regular basis about how we have ministered to others when we had no idea we did anything. We have simply stayed involved with the same activities such as Little League, church, and PTA. This past October, we hosted a golf tournament to benefit the Eric Head Memorial Scholarship Fund that was established at his high school. The turnout was incredible—eighty-six people played golf in the wind and rain. They raised $8,000 for the fund. This has been one way for us to stay involved and keep his memory alive. Your comments about allowing others to minister to you and your family really made sense to me."

Jonathan and Glenda Head have gotten over it in the sense that they have moved on. Their pain is there; it will always be there. But they have done something wonderful in the midst of their pain. They have kept their son's name alive through the memorial fund.

Something else in Jonathan's e-mail struck me. They learned the influence of their son's life on others. I can think of no greater tribute to a person's time on earth than to realize how he or she had touched other lives.

All of us have an inborn desire to leave a legacy behind—to say to the world, "Hey, I was here." Eric did that—and he did it without realizing the impact he made.

If we live long enough, we all lose people we love. I talk to people constantly who have lost loved ones. Death is painful for the ones left behind and it's important to mourn our losses, but too many people don't move beyond that.

We have to get past the mourning stage. Yes, we need to acknowledge the loss and separation but we must also celebrate life.

If we remain, we must have something to do. God has a purpose in our staying. In the case of Eric Head, none of us can understand why he died. But he did. His parents have found purpose in their lives through their grief.

Another example of someone who "got over it" is Tammy Kelley, a young woman who e-mailed me: "I am a person with a disability, and I have often thanked God for my disability. I use my condition to make contact with other people with any kind of disability, not just the same one I have. I thought that it would make them more comfortable and I could also offer encouragement. I learned a long time ago that having Parkinson's disease doesn't define me, but being a Christian does. I have faced adversity since the day I was born. I was born three months early and weighed only twenty-two ounces. I was a twin, but my sibling didn't survive. I have known since I was a teenager that God had a purpose for having me not go to heaven with my twin, but I don't know what that purpose is."

Although Tammy doesn't seem to know her purpose, I think she is serving that purpose by reaching out to others. She has gotten over it—in the positive sense—and uses her life and the reality of her own limited physical world to reach out to others and say to them, "You aren't alone. God is with you and there are people like me who care."

"Have you forgiven the driver of the truck that ran you over?" To my surprise, I get that question quite often. It makes me wonder why so many people ask. I believe the driver of the truck swerved into my lane because he wasn't a good driver, probably had never driven a truck before, and didn't know what he was doing. The prison officials should never have allowed him to take the wheel. He did drive, and he hit me, but I have never believed that he purposely tried to harm me.

I firmly believe in forgiveness. Whenever we pray the Lord's Prayer, we ask God to forgive us as we have forgiven.

Paul wrote to the Ephesians, "Get rid of all bitterness, rage and anger . . . forgiving each other, just as in Christ God forgave you" (Ephesians 4:31 and 32b[†]).

As Christians, forgiving isn't an option. It may not be easy, but it's the right thing to do. It's for our own good as well as for the good of the other. When we don't forgive, it's like a knot in our stomach that never goes away and just gets stronger.

Yes, I have unreservedly forgiven the driver. In my case, it wasn't difficult. In fact, I never saw it as an intentional act or an attempt to hurt me. I've never spoken to him. Once I was physically well enough to make contact, I learned he had been released and had moved out of the area. I would have liked to talk to him, but his address was confidential information and I couldn't get permission to contact him. I would have liked to ask, "Will you tell me about what happened back there? How did the accident occur?"

I don't blame him or hold anything against him. If there is any blame, it's for those who gave him the keys. But again, no one wanted to hurt me. It was one of those things that we can't explain. It's like the pilot who unintentionally flew down the wrong runway or the air traffic controller whose attention was diverted. The results were horrific, but the motives were not bad.

Some people, of course, blame God for every bad thing that happens. But it's rather strange and inconsistent, because those same people don't give God praise when good things happen.

When we hold anger at God or anyone, it means we refuse to look at ourselves and examine our own hearts. We refuse to move out of our pain. It's as if we yell to the world around us, "This is my pain. I'm entitled to it, and I'm going to stick with it." No one says those words, but that's their attitude.

When I speak to bitter and angry people I try to nudge them to move on. Instead of asking, "Why is God doing this to me?" I want them to ask, "What can God do through my life as a result of this tragedy or pain?"

We need to learn to stop complaining and stop shaking our fist at God. Incidentally we can't intimidate God. We can be as angry as we want, and he has one simple message for us, "I love you and I'll always love you."

Being angry with God won't change anything. In the Bible, Jonah was angry at God and grumbled. So did Elijah. But their anger changed nothing and it never stopped God from loving them.

Thus the real question is, "What can I learn from this?" or "What's my purpose now?" One of the great joys I experience in my travels is that I meet those individuals who have gotten over it. They have used their pain and their heartbreak to help others who hurt.

One woman told me she had founded a support group for families of children who overdosed on drugs. She used her brokenhearted experience to reach out to others and in the process, she moved on. She has helped many others go through the mourning and hurt that she endured.

I'll give you an example. Lisa (not her real name) had to walk two blocks from the bus stop to her apartment. Because she worked long hours, some evenings she had to walk down a badly lit street.

Four men abducted her and each of them raped her. She said it was two years before she could stand to have anyone touch her in any way. At the time of the rape, she was twenty-one years old, newly married, and had a career lined up with a marketing firm. By age twenty-three, she was divorced, jobless, and emotionally empty. She almost took her own life and seriously contemplated it for more than a month. But Lisa had been brought up in the church and believed suicide was wrong.

In her despair, she talked to the pastor of a local church and underwent counseling for almost a year. She joined a group of survivors of sexual assault. Because of the help she received, today Lisa has become a therapist whose specialty is helping rape victims.

"For years I hated those men. Every day I prayed for God to kill them," she said. "So far as I know, none of them have ever been caught, but I stopped praying for their deaths and began to pray for my life. They had made me the victim once. If I continued to hold on to my hatred, I would be a victim a second time— maybe remain a victim for life."

Lisa's testimony is what I mean by getting over it. It's not leaving the pain behind, but it's growing from the pain and using what we have to help and encourage others.

After my recovery from the accident, I was in transition. I couldn't go back to the old way of life. In my case, I couldn't go back physically. Others can't return to the old ways for other reasons.

In fact, living the new normal means there is no going back. There is either standing still or moving forward.

I've found comfort in the words of the apostle Paul to the Philippians. He spoke of himself: "I don't mean to say that . . . I have already reached perfection. But I press on to possess that perfection for which Christ Jesus first possessed me. No, dear brothers and sisters, I have not achieved it, but I focus on this one thing: Forgetting the past and looking forward to what lies ahead" (Philippians 3:12–13**).

That's the attitude I want to continue to cultivate. Although I changed after my accident and I became more open to people, it still took years before I reached out as I have now. My accident happened in 1989. After two years I finally talked about my accident and my trip to heaven. That was a big factor in getting over the past and stretching forward.

How could I ever have dreamed of what doors God would open for me? I was an average pastor in a suburb of Houston. I had no idea that I would travel across the world with a simple message of hope and encouragement. But I had to get over the past before I could move into the future. I was finally able to open up and talk freely about heaven.

This is the third book my coauthor and I have written. Since the first book came out in the fall of 2004, I've spoken to millions of people all over the world. I had a heavenly experience, but it was more than an experience. It was more than living with physical limitations. I could offer others the hope and the assurance that heaven is a real place and a place for them to choose.

Have I gotten over "it"? Absolutely. I still suffer with pain and am daily aware of my physical limitations, but I have found my purpose. It's not the purpose I would have chosen, but it's what

God has given me to do and I want to remain faithful to the task as long as I have the strength to do so.

Some days when I stand up in churches to speak, I'm physically and emotionally exhausted. It takes everything I have just to stand in front of a congregation. I have a terrible problem with circulation in my legs; my feet swell severely when I fly on planes or drive long distances to the various cities and countries for meetings. Just to put on my socks and tie my shoes is often a real challenge. But I keep on because I believe this is what God wants me to do.

On some of those occasions, I wish I were home in my own bed or sitting across the table from my wife, Eva. Some days I wonder why I do what I do. But I go ahead and I speak. Somehow God provides the energy.

Afterward is my payment—after I speak and some members of the audience make me know it was worth the effort. "Your message tonight changed my life." Or individuals will wait around until everyone has gone and open their hearts to me. They want to turn their lives around—to get over it—and they wait to tell me about it.

They come to me for help. That still amazes me. When I look back to 1989 and the long months of recovery, I could never, never have envisioned that anyone would ever come to me for help in such a variety of ways. But I've learned that's one of the great miracles of getting over it—we never know what God will do with us or through us.

Sometimes I reflect on others who have moved beyond their pain. None of them chose their form of helping others. But if it hadn't been for their tragedies, they would never have been exposed to the needs that they can now help alleviate, like Kelly, who reaches out to those with disability, or the woman who ministers to families that have lost children through drug overdoses.

To "get over it" means to make a transition, and we have to be open to opportunities that will make our pain and our hurt matter. Doesn't it make more sense to take the circumstances of our lives and use them to help someone else? It's certainly better than to wallow in the quagmire of despair. Doesn't it make more sense to find inner peace by helping others find healing? I think it does. I also say it this way: It actually takes more energy—a lot more—to remain bitter or angry. It takes less energy to transfer those emotions into something positive, and we become instruments of healing.

NINE

New Markers

A man came to one of my meetings and spoke to me at length about his situation. I don't remember his name or if he even told it to me, so I'll call him Pat.

Pat lost his job because the company merged with another organization. His employer gave him a generous severance package and said, "This should take care of you until you find a new position."

Pat gave his boss the brightest smile he could plaster on his face, but as he walked out of the office, he thought, I'm fifty-six years old. I've worked here for nearly thirty years. Now what do I do?

When we talked, Pat had been out of work for seven months and his severance package was almost used up. "I'll probably never be able to find a job like the one I had. I had worked my way upward. If I can even find a good job, I know I'll make only a fraction of what I earned at my old company." He also said that he was aware of age discrimination, even if no one used those words.

His eyes filled with tears as he related his experience. Like so many others, Pat said, "I never saw it coming." The merger had been in the planning stage for a long time, of course, but the executives said nothing to the workers. Pat heard about the merger about two weeks before the people who worked under him. "My boss, the vice president, assured me that no matter what happened, I'd still have a job." Pat shook his head. "They let him go before I got the axe."

Pat's lifestyle has changed. He can never go back to the way life was before. He has to find a new normal.

I've told this story to illustrate that things happen to us— things that irrevocably alter our lives. Most of the time we initially respond with shock. "How could this happen to me?" We're thrown into confusion and we have to struggle to maintain our balance. We're forced to make decisions about who we are and where we're going.

One woman named Jennifer, whose husband died after twenty-three years of marriage, said, "I don't even know who I am anymore. I'm no longer a wife. Our only son is in college and doesn't need me. I've been so tuned in to those two people, I've forgotten who I am, and now I'm forced to find out."

The widow, Jennifer, and Pat, the downsized businessman, and I—all of us have faced those forced changes. Circumstances modify our lives and we can't do things the way we did before. None of us likes to be pushed into the place where we have to act, especially when we're not prepared. But then, the most traumatic moments often come when we least expect them.

We sometimes call that the locker-room mentality. Players and coaches go into the locker room before every game and again at halftime and they work through their game plans. "This is what we're going to make happen."

And maybe events will happen that way.

The implication is that they decide what will take place before they get out on the field. They know, however, that they can plan, but they can't predict what will actually happen. When they play against another team, they may end up defeated and cry about the outcome. They also realize that (as one person put it), "All you can do is all you can do."

But life does throw us curve balls. Our plans go awry. People fail us. Accidents happen. Regardless of the cause, life changes. Some psychologists refer to those things as *markers*. A marker can be something as simple as the first time a girl wears makeup. When teens receive their driver's licenses, it's a marker. It can be the breakup of a marriage or death of a friend. Regardless of what happens, our lives are irrevocably affected, sometimes dramatically, sometimes less so. Regardless of the extent, life becomes different.

We have markers all through life. There are those times that shout, "A new chapter in life begins here!" Some of them may be joyful, such as marriage or the birth of a child or the first grandchild or graduating from college. No matter what the situation, change takes place and we have to move into a new normal.

I particularly want to focus on what we think of as the negative markers. If we persist and if we continue in our growth, at some point we are able to look back and see those same markers as positive. We can't rush the process, but the moment comes when we can even pause to give thanks to God for those events. Some people never reach that place, of course.

In one sense, trauma is trauma whether it's

- the man who lost his job,
- the woman who got shot in the face during a robbery,
- the couple who lost their child to a drowning,
- the woman who lost her son in Iraq,
- the man whose wife left him or the woman whose husband left her,
- the parents who refuse to speak to their children because of something they have done, or
- the huge financial disasters that befell a family.

All of the above situations are disasters. And all of them are markers in life.

Regardless of what we call it, as soon as we realize we have a new marker, we have to reconfigure our lives. If we had an income of $100,000 last year and this year we must subsist on one-fourth of that amount, we must do a lot of difficult, painful rethinking of how we spend money.

We may have known what we wanted to do if life had continued as it was, but the rules have all changed. The markers have forced us to make a new game plan.

Markers have to do with the past, the present, and the future. We live in the present but we have a past. Too many people want to go backward and live there—live in the old ways—but that's impossible. Even though everyone knows it, some people just can't let go. They say, "The way it was supposed to be . . ." Growth means we acknowledge the past, accept the present, but look to the future.

One thing I want to point out is this: There must be an accepted end before there can be a new beginning. And there's usually an important empty time between the two. It's the time when we try to make sense of what hit us, especially when we had no warning.

I had months of time in the hospital to do that. I didn't understand the cause or have any idea of what would happen after I left the hospital, but I went through the time of emptiness. I knew who I had been, but I didn't know who I would become.

I think of my friend Yvonne Ortega, who faced a terrible period of her life. She and her husband divorced, she had a teenage son to raise alone, and she had to teach full time to pay her bills. Her son graduated from high school, joined the military, and she thought life would calm down and become simpler. However, in a routine self-examination, she found a lump in her breast. It was cancer.

She survived, but Yvonne says that for months she just did what she had to do and felt empty and alone. That's the in-between time. Later she would minister to other women with cancer through her book, *Hope for the Journey Through Cancer: Inspiration for Each Day*.[2] Cancer became her new marker, but it didn't define her. It wasn't the life she had asked for, but it became a life that is now fuller than it ever was before.

"God is real," she says. "I was a Christian before that, but I went through severe spiritual testing. I'm stronger today, and I know heaven is real and it's the home I'll inherit when I leave this life. But it wasn't always like that."

People struggle with those markers and changes in their lives. When they go through that empty period, they sometimes feel as

---

[2] *Hope for the Journey Through Cancer* (Grand Rapids: Revell, 2007).

if God has deserted them, they've abandoned God, or they're too confused to know what's going on with themselves. From my own experience, I know that emptiness means really empty. It means we feel as if there is nothing from which to pull. But emptiness doesn't last—it's a temporary place after the new marker.

To help people with this, here's a question I sometimes pose: Where were you the closest to God?

If you can find out where that place is, that's probably where you need to start again. You need to go back, examine that marker, and realize that the rules of the game have changed. You have to venture out, but now you do so under new conditions. If you can begin at the marker—at the turning point—at that bridge—you can look at your defeats and failures and say, "I don't have to make the same kind of mistakes again."

The new markers are there like a signpost to say, "The road you once traveled on has been permanently closed. Ahead is your new road and you must follow it until you come to the next new marker."

Once we've accepted that new marker, we can think positively in the present. When we're overwhelmed by events or circumstances we usually can't think positively. When Pat said, "I never saw it coming," he wasn't able to think positively for quite a while. He tried to come to terms with the drastic change of events. He said that for weeks, he wanted to go back to work at the same place. He wasn't willing to work through the emptiness. He would look backward at the way things had been—or the way he perceived them to have been. Until he said, "I have to move on with my new life," he hadn't accepted the new marker.

Too many refuse to see that the end has come or to admit the need for an ending of the old. Letting go can be hard—very hard. It's as if no matter how bad things were in the past, that state of emptiness will be worse. Some part of us holds us back. No matter what our heads tell us, our hearts want our old way of life back.

A nurse told me that after eighteen years of marriage her husband left her. For the next year, she went to work, came home, and spent most of the time in bed. "I wanted him back. He was the love of my life and when he left, so did all meaning."

She remained in a state of emptiness until she came to face the reality of her circumstances. He was never going to come back. "He may have been the love of my life," she said, "but I wasn't his. Just to say that sentence aloud every day for weeks slowly brought me out of my depression. I had been largely defined by my roles and relationships, both those I liked and those I didn't like."

Many of us know we need to change but we don't want to change. When we're forced to cross a bridge, the transitional situation seems to leave us with little choice. We can, of course, continue to regret and grumble, but to make the most of the situation we're forced to look at the negative and the positive aspects of our new situation.

As the nurse compared the past with the present, the present was deficient and heartbreaking. But she was finally able to say, "I won't let this defeat me. I don't know how I can handle life as it is, but I'll do it." That woman was finally able to say, "He was my life, but that life is gone. Now I have my own life and I've decided to make the most of it."

Once she made the commitment to see her life—her present life—as a reality and see that she couldn't go backward, she was ready to move on. Today, she works six months in a hospital as a critical care nurse. She spends the other six months in third world countries where she can use her skills to help others. "I never realized how wonderful life could be," she said.

I've met too many people who never want to move beyond the past, but most of us, however, finally determine that we won't be defeated. In some form, we finally say, "I might be knocked down but I'm not going to be knocked out." We look ahead, and we set new goals. Epictetus, an ancient Roman philosopher, once wrote, "What ought one to say then as each hardship comes? I was practicing for this, I was training for this."

That's true, but most of us can't say those words, at least not at first and perhaps not for many years. We feel our pain and hardship. We struggle with life's unfairness. Once we realize— emotionally—that we can't reclaim the past, but that we can learn from it, our attitudes change. Sometimes we see mistakes we've made and we promise ourselves never to make them again. At other times we have no awareness of failure or wrongdoing—and there may not be any. We just have to learn to adapt to our new normal.

After my accident, I had many lessons to learn. For example, I had to learn to accept help from others because I could no longer rely only on myself. Could I have learned those lessons in other ways? Of course, but that is the method God used to open my eyes to my need and to teach me compassion toward others.

Markers show where we've been. When understood properly, they also point ahead as if to say, "Follow this new path. It's safe because God is with you."

We all need markers. We may remember them and we may

occasionally look back at the huge signposts that say, "This is where you changed directions. This is where you began the new normal." It's all right to have reminders of where we have been, but if we're wise, we use those markers as ways to measure our progress. We can look back and say, "That's who I used to be. Thank God for who I am now."

TEN

Focusing on the Eternal

I started this book by using the image of crossing bridges as a way to help explain the way life changes for all of us. We all have bridges we must cross. Most of us aren't even aware that they're bridges. We expect life to go on as it did before. What we have to face is that things happen and life can never be the same. The old life—the old way—is gone. We must find a new normal.

That search isn't easy. First we face the difficult process of letting go of the old—the way things were. No matter how much we want to hold onto life as it was, once we cross a bridge things change—we change. We have to recognize our life will never be the same.

As challenging as that is, the next step is even more agonizing. Letting go of our old life is like jumping off of a cliff into empty, dark nothingness. We're leaving behind the familiar and stepping into the unknown. We know we must find a new way of looking at life, but we don't know exactly what to do. It's a time of suffering and confusion.

People talk to me and say things such as, "I seem to have crossed some kind of threshold in life. There's no turning back. My old life is gone. But I don't know what to do now. People tell me I have to move on, find a new direction, and I realize that, but I'm still mourning my old life, and right now, I just don't know what else to do."

I often respond with something like this: "Every transition begins with an ending. We have to let go of the old before we start the new. But it's not as easy as hitting a switch. It's a process, and we have to go through the darkness before we emerge on the other side. The key is to use the time well, shifting our focus so instead of looking inward, bemoaning what we've lost and trying to figure out how we can deal with it, we begin to look outward, to someone who can heal us, guide us, and give us strength for our journey. Instead of asking, 'How am I going to live without my old life?' we begin to ask, 'How am I going to live with my new life?' And in doing so, we will discover the path God is laying before us, the purpose He has for our lives."

After my accident, as I lay in my hospital bed, I struggled through the darkness. I was in physical pain, I had permanent disabilities, and I knew I would never be the same man I was when I started driving across the Livingston Bridge. I was angry and felt sorry for myself. All I could think about was what I lost: I was no longer the man my wife, Eva, married. There were things I would never be physically able to do with my kids. And even though I had spent ninety minutes in heaven, this felt like another loss. Why would God give me a peek of paradise only to bring me back here a suffering, broken man?

It took a while before I discovered my new normal and even longer to find the purpose in my pain. I'm still amazed at the impact my story has on people, and although I still long for that perfection that is heaven, I know I'm doing exactly what God intends for me to do.

As I travel the world sharing my message of hope, I meet many people who have crossed a bridge and emerged on the other side with a greater sense of purpose. But you don't have to look further than the Bible for some stunning examples. Immediately I think of Paul, the great apostle and writer of the Bible. Before he became a Christian he was a religious man and a devout follower of the Law of Moses. One day, on his way to capture, imprison, and kill Christians, he fell down on the road, totally blind. This was a bridge for him, and his life would never be the same. He could have refused to turn to the Lord, but he listened, prayed, was healed, and became a leading force in proclaiming God's love to the world.

As powerful as that was—and I don't want to minimize this event—the second bridge Paul crossed became even more powerful. This was the bridge that gave Paul his life's purpose.

People may not notice this second major turning point in Paul's life. It's veiled but it's there. In 2 Corinthians 11, Paul writes at length about his suffering. Within this book he makes such statements as: "I have . . . been exposed to death again and again . . . (2 Corinthians 11:23†). He writes of being "caught up in the third heaven" (2 Corinthians 12:2†) and "was caught up to paradise" (2 Corinthians 12:4†).

No one truly knows what he meant by the third heaven. He says little about the experience except that "he was caught up to paradise" and "he heard inexpressible things, things that man is not permitted to tell" (12:4†).

Because of my ninety minutes in heaven, I believe Paul had an experience of heaven. Did he die as I did? Did he have a near-death experience? Was it a vision of such power that he temporarily lost all sense of reality in his life?

None of us know, but he had an absolutely glorious experience. When he wrote to the Philippians, he wrote of his great struggle: "For to me, to live is Christ and to die is gain. . . . Yet what shall I choose? I do not know! I am torn between the two: I desire to depart and be with Christ, which is better by far; but it is more necessary for you that I remain in the body" (Philippians 1:21–24).

After that experience, Paul also wrote about a thorn in the flesh. Most scholars believe it was some kind of physical limitation. Whatever it was, he was different after his journey to the third heaven. Inwardly he was stronger than he had ever been; outwardly he had diminished.

I don't want to compare myself with Paul, but I believe he experienced as much or more than I did. He tasted enough of the heavenly glory that he wanted to stay. Every day he wanted to return—just as I still do. But each day, he also realized that God wasn't ready for him to leave this earth, so he stayed for the sake of the people he could help. That was what he was here to do.

We can see another example of this transition in the apostle Peter. Jesus called him and his companions to leave their fishing nets and follow Him. Peter followed Jesus and this can certainly be seen as a bridge in his life. But the bridge where I think Peter found his life's purpose is recorded in Luke 5. Apparently Peter and his friends continued to fish. One day, Jesus came along and saw their boats were empty. He told Simon Peter to go out deeper, let down the nets, and they would catch many fish. " 'Master,' Simon replied, 'we worked hard all last night and didn't catch a thing. But if you say so, I'll let the nets down again' " (Verse 5**). They did and caught enough for two boats to overflow.

Here's where Peter's bridge comes in: "When Simon Peter realized what had happened, he fell to his knees before Jesus and said, 'Oh, Lord, please leave me—I'm too much of a sinner to be around you.' For he was awestruck by the number of fish they had caught, as were the others with him" (Verses 8–9). Peter didn't think he was worthy and fell down, not knowing what to do with himself. "Jesus replied to Simon, 'Don't be afraid! From now on you'll be fishing for people'" (Verse 10b). At that moment, Peter knows what his purpose in life is.

A third example can be found in the life of Jesus, himself. Jesus crossed a bridge immediately after his baptism. "A voice from heaven said, 'This is my Son, whom I love; with him I am well pleased'" (Matthew 3:17†). That's a powerful experience, but the next verse reads, "Then Jesus was led by the Spirit into the desert to be tempted by the devil" (4:1). If Jesus ever had a new normal experience, that's where it began. Until that moment, he was the son of Joseph, a carpenter in Nazareth. After that day, he was Jesus, the Messiah. His life changed forever between his baptism and the forty days of temptation. He entered the desert in obedience and emerged as the herald of God's good news.

Of course, there is also the most significant of bridges that Jesus crossed. He went from being the Great Teacher and the Healer to become the Savior. His death on the cross was the last bridge for him to cross. His entire life had led to that great moment when he gave his life as a substitute for others.

All of us cross bridges that change our lives. One such person is Jennifer Lasiter, who e-mailed me a few months after she had to cross a bridge of great pain. Her letter was not about the pain or how horrible life had become, but about what life was like on the other side of that bridge.

"I have always been a Christian, always had faith in God, and always believed that I would go to heaven. Recently I've gone through several difficult and painful changes in my life. Several special people in my life have died. One lost her life in a car accident and she was only twenty-one. Another friend was twenty-three and she died from a drug overdose. During that same period of time, I lost a grandparent. Those times were especially hard for me. The one thing that brought me peace was that they were in heaven and 'in a better place' (as people often say). Your description of heaven made it so much easier for me to bear the loss of these loved ones. I have deep peace knowing where they are.

"Those events have caused me to do some soul-searching and to take time for myself and reflect on the past. I want to learn from my mistakes and make positive changes. One of the big realizations for me has been that although I was a Christian and a believer, I was living my life selfishly and not living for God.

"A couple of months ago, I rededicated my life to Jesus and am learning to include him in everything I do and to live my life according to his will.

"I am a nurse in the Surgical Intensive Care Unit (SICU) at Louisiana State University Medical Center in Shreveport. This is the only Level I trauma unit in the whole state of Louisiana. I've seen so many people brought in after horrible car accidents. Several have had injuries such as yours and had to have an external fixator. As I work with them and witness their suffering and their pain, I think of your story. You found new hope and meaning in a seemingly hopeless situation.

"In the ICU, we seldom get to see the final results of what we do because, as you well know, people are usually still very sick with a lot of healing and rehab before them when they leave the ICU. After reading your story, I have renewed faith and hope, and I'm inspired to do the best I can for these people, though I can't see the final results.

"Five years ago, one of my friends passed away and her mother has had a difficult time with that loss. I plan to give her your book because I know it will give her more of a sense of peace to know about heaven and where her daughter is.

"As I write you, my grandfather is ill and on his last round of chemotherapy for lung cancer. I think that he'll make that journey soon and I want to ease his fears about dying.

"I feel I can use your book and your story to help people in many ways. I am pretty sure that everyone needs to read it for one reason or another. I think it has so much to offer in so many ways. I am recommending it to everyone I know!

"In fact, I want to give copies of your books to my ICU patients and their families to help them through their recoveries and inspire them. Most of all, I'd like to touch those people who are just like I used to be—the people who have 'one foot in the world and one foot in the church.' I also want to share your story with those who don't know God and to show them that they can change."

Jennifer's story shows us that she crossed a bridge and her life took on new meaning—and now she had determined to make her life count for others.

The issue we have to face—and the one that may be the most difficult—is that we have crossed over the bridge, and we're on the other side. Now we have to ask ourselves: What is the focus of our lives? Where are we going? We know where we've been. In some ways, we liked it and we may have found it enjoyable, even wonderful. But we can never go back. We're at the great threshold of life and we know the only way to go is to move ahead.

Where is our focus now? We know where we don't want to be: languishing in self-pity and alienated from ourselves. But where do we want to be? Where do we go?

Given the constraints of what we now have to work with, which may include physical disabilities and certainly the pain of loss, confusion, and anger over what we went through, we still have to make a choice: What is our new focus? If we're wise, we move from a temporal perspective to an eternal perspective. Peter did this in that powerful moment of realization that he was a great sinner. Paul came back from the third heaven and he couldn't be the same. Even Jesus, the perfect man, had to face the fact that he had a destiny that he had to fulfill.

So do we all. What is yours?

ELEVEN

The Heavenly Perspective

I find that the people who seem to be most content in life are those who find and maintain an eternal perspective. Even if they've been through horrible circumstances and live with terrible disabilities, they are able to get the most meaning from their lives. They can do that because they've shifted from the present darkness and pain and are able to focus on what lies ahead for them. They seem to have meaningful and purposeful lives.

Paul told persecuted Christians (and it's just as true for knocked-down Christians today), "Yet what we suffer now is nothing compared to the glory he will reveal to us later" (Romans 8:18**).

That's what I mean by a heavenly perspective. We need to realize where we're going now—as much as we can—but we always keep our eyes on the final bridge we must cross. Heaven is real and we will go there, but God wants us to have a little bit of heaven here on this earth. I like to think of that as preparation for the end.

Think about it. When we became believers, God could have zapped us right up to heaven. I believe that part of the reason we remain is for us to influence others. But we're also here for ourselves. God wants us to enjoy our lives. He wants us to walk with Jesus while we're here on earth. As long as we're alive, God's loving hand reaches out to us and asks us to turn to Jesus Christ. We might come at sixteen or forty-eight or eighty-eight. When we come isn't as important as the reality of that decision. One of the thieves on the cross next to Jesus turned to him before he died. He's in heaven now, but he had no opportunity to join the bit of heaven available on earth.

David said it this way: "Taste and see that the Lord is good. Oh, the joys of those who take refuge in him!" (Psalm 34:8).

While I stress the joy of heaven, one of the things some people don't understand is that the joy is for now—not just for eternity. I'm delighted every time I learn of anyone who turns to God. But there's also a sadness when we know some of them won't be on earth long enough to enjoy that bit of heaven.

For example, in the early summer I was in a church in England and gave the invitation to turn to Jesus Christ. A number of people responded. I especially noticed three individuals. Each of them was obviously more than seventy years old.

I've been a preacher for thirty years. In my entire lifetime I have never before seen three elderly people come forward in the same service to say, "We want to become Christians."

One of them, named Donald, talked to me. He walked with a cane and was slightly stooped. He took my hand and shook it. That's when I noticed tears in his eyes.

"I am so happy for you, Donald, that you made the most important decision you'll ever make."

"It is important, isn't it?"

"Absolutely. Without question, the most important."

"I'm so happy." His face glowed when he said those words. "This is the happiest day of my life."

"I'm happy for you," I said. We talked for several minutes, and I said, "I look forward to seeing you one day in heaven."

"Thank God he let me live long enough to do this."

"That's right! We need to thank God for that."

But as I said those words, I thought, Donald, you lived all these years and God gave you still another chance. I hope others won't presume that they have all the time in the world. Now is the time.

Donald now has a heavenly perspective. I wish he had found that perspective sixty or seventy years ago. He feels he's close to heaven physically—and he is—but he has also started to live close to heaven spiritually.

Donald's story goes to show, it's never too late to get closer to heaven. Here's another example of what I'm talking about:

"I serve a local nursing home and present Bible studies every other Saturday morning," wrote Elizabeth Ann Starr. "Time and time again, God has plans that quite often surprise us. As I was visiting nursing homes for my mother's placement, I noted whether Bible study was an activity that was offered. After we decided on Apple Valley, I realized they had a number of church services, but no Bible study.

"God took over my heart for those dear people and shortly afterward I started a Bible study. We have met for nearly three years. At a study we might have as few as four residents or as many as sixteen. Some don't say a word, some cry, some contribute and often ask questions.

"About a month ago, one of the women, fairly new to our group, brought up the process of dying and heaven. There was a real longing in that woman's eyes to understand more fully what would happen. Nancy is 94 years old! My heart was so touched and I knew that had to be the message for our next meeting. I had quite a number of Scripture verses but felt I needed something else—something that would help all of them to have a deeper understanding, knowledge, peace, and assurance about what God promises those who believe in him. As I entered a local Christian bookstore, a shelf to my left caught my eye and your book *90 Minutes in Heaven* was prominently displayed. I was so surprised at the title and wondered what that was about.

"I thumbed through the first few pages, and I knew it was my answer to prayer. I read the entire book that evening and find it hard to express in words what I experienced. My brochure for the morning (that I always prepare and give them) was all Scripture verses. I highlighted most of the parts of your story that I wanted to read to them—I have never done that before because many of them have short attention spans and hearing losses. But I felt I could only retell your story by using your own words, so I read them.

"To say it was a powerful morning is inadequate to describe the presence and work of the Holy Spirit. Just as you said in your story numerous times, it feels very awkward to try to put human words to divine experiences!

"Nancy was in tears and so thankful for what I brought to the study. 'I believe God wanted him to live so that we could hear about heaven this morning,' she said.

"I reminded them of Lazarus and that Jesus raised him from the dead to glorify God and increase their faith.

"I give thanks to God for your life, your ministry, your story and all the sacrifices you have made so that others' faith may be increased."

Once we make that decision to follow Jesus Christ, our lives need to reflect it. It's interesting how much the Bible has to say about our behavior. God rewards our actions now but even more when we reach the heavenly portals.

The rewards of heaven won't happen until the end, but we can prepare ourselves for those rewards. Let's reflect on one of Jesus' famous stories, that of the sheep and the goats found in Matthew 25.

Jesus says that on the Day of Judgment, he'll separate people like sheep and goats. The sheep will be on his right hand and they are the blessed.

"Then the King will say to those on the right, 'Come, you who are blessed by my Father, inherit the Kingdom prepared for you from the creation of the world. For I was hungry, and you fed me. I was thirsty, and you gave me a drink. I was a stranger, and you invited me into your home. I was naked, and you gave me clothing. I was sick, and you cared for me. I was in prison, and you visited me'" (Verses 34–36**). He also went on to point out that many won't realize they did that for him: "And the King will say, 'I tell you the truth, when you did it to one of the least of these my brothers and sisters, you were doing it to me!'" (Verse 40).

That's the part of the reality of heaven I eagerly await—and I hope that's true with all of us. That will be the time when we receive rewards in heaven for our faithfulness on earth.

Once we make the decision on earth to serve Jesus Christ, we need to live out that decision by the kind of things mentioned previously. I believe that as much as the things we do for others, we also need to exude our relationship to God. When we manifest joy, peace, acceptance, love, and understanding, that's also how we serve others—by being a living example of the perfection of heaven.

I've experienced the reality and I'm zealous about this, but I want everyone to know not only that heaven is real, but it is a wonderful, perfect place. When I was a child and my parents told us kids we were going to Grandma's house, we got excited. We jumped around and clapped and yelled. It was a big thing to make a trip to Grandma's house.

I think of my children today. One of my sons, Joe, is the kind of kid who's laid-back and doesn't seem to be in a hurry for anything. But I remember once when I said, "We're going to go to Disney World," he was eager to go. He counted days and constantly reminded me of my promise to take him there.

That's how I see heaven. It's not just the future place to go, but it's where we go with a strong sense of joyful expectation.

And you know what? We set dates for trips to Disney World or Six Flags, but there's one thing we can't set a date for—the day we leave this world. That's not the kind of information any of us has access to. In the past few years, I've spoken with thousands who thought a loved one would live longer. They were sure Dad would recover or a friend would survive. But they took a sudden downturn and died.

I buried my aunt three weeks from the day her husband died. We stood at the same cemetery at the same hour in the same place with an identical funeral. We had no reason to believe that she would go that quickly. But she did. Who would have known? Who could have predicted?

We never know when we will cross that final bridge, and if we want to be in heaven when we get to the other side, we have to be prepared. Part of that preparation, Jesus made clear, is to have a heavenly perspective. We live here and do our best while we look "homeward." Jesus put it this way: "Don't store up treasures here on earth. . . . Store your treasures in heaven. . . . Wherever your treasure is, there the desires of your heart will also be" (Matthew 6:19–21**). His point is not against having things or enjoying the good things in this life. His point is that wherever we put our treasure—our energies and our time—that's where our hearts and thoughts are.

The heavenly perspective isn't about possessions or lack of them, but about an *attitude* that sees life here on earth as preparation for the glorious life to come. If our hearts are in tune with God and we seek to be guided by the Holy Spirit, that's the heavenly perspective.

There's a story about a famous preacher at a baccalaureate service who stared at the graduates for several seconds. When he opened his mouth, the first sentence was, "One of these days you're going to die."

I'm sure some people asked themselves, "What kind of graduation speech is this?"

He went on to say, "One of these days you're going to die and after you die they're going to take you out and bury you and then come back to the house and sit on the front porch and eat potato salad."

Graduation speeches are usually about our future, and I'm sure he did that to make them think about the real future. The preacher went on to say something like this: "When you were born, everyone was happy. A new child was born and they were excited. How will people feel when you die? Will they be sad? Will they miss you? Did it matter that you lived?"

It's all a matter of how you lived your life. Do you want to be remembered for what you did for yourself—how much money you made, the kind of car you drove, the size of the house you lived in? Or do you want people to remember what you did for others—your kindness and compassion; your generosity of time, money, and spirit; the testimony you freely shared to bring others to Christ? I suspect more people would lovingly recall the memory of those latter virtues, and I know without a doubt which option would most please the Lord.

There's a famous but anonymous saying that goes like this: "When you were born, you cried and the world rejoiced. Live your life so that when you die, you will rejoice and the world will cry."

That's the choice we have from the time we're born until we die. We live in what someone has called the hyphen of life. Our tombstones are generally etched with our name, the date of our birth, and the date of our death. The hyphen that separates the dates of our birth and death is our entire lives. How we live it determines where we will end up when we cross the final bridge.

As I think about the tombstone, I'm strongly reminded of an incident in my own life—an experience I've never forgotten and one that has taken on special meaning for me since my accident.

When I was thirteen years old, my father's mother died. It was the first funeral I ever attended. My dad was on his way overseas on a troop ship to Korea and we couldn't make contact with him, so he couldn't attend the funeral. My mother, my brothers, and I went, and we were heartbroken over the loss.

Grandma Piper had lived in Arkansas and the interment was at a rural cemetery behind an old white clapboard church. Hundreds came because she had a very large family. My dad is one of eleven kids and many of them had thirteen children, so it's a huge family.

After the funeral, we started toward the gravesite, which is up a hill behind the church. I walked by myself—I'm not sure why that happened, but I was alone. I noticed I was in a section with a lot of tombstones for various members of the Piper family.

Then I saw the tombstone that read: Larry Donald Piper. That's my full name, Larry Donald Piper.

In shock, I stopped and stared. I was only thirteen, but I was totally stunned. I couldn't seem to move on. I just stared at that stone with my name etched on it.

Just then a hand gripped my shoulder. I turned around; my aunt Maxine had come up behind me.

"Honey, we need to get up to the grave. We don't want to be late."

She was wrong. I wanted to be late. I didn't want to go up there. I never wanted to go up there. So she kept patting my shoulder and said several times, "We need to go now. We need to go."

I shook my head. I was in such shock I couldn't speak.

Just then she looked down and read the tombstone. "Oh, that's your name, isn't it?"

I nodded, unable to speak.

She thought for a moment and then she said, "Oh, I know. Your aunt Mildred had a little a boy that died at birth and that was his name. This is where he's buried. He has the same name as you."

I nodded again and finally I moved on. At least I understood that tombstone wasn't *mine*.

I've never forgotten that tombstone. I can close my eyes and see it yet today and say, "There's a tombstone in Arkansas with my name on it." It may not be mine, but the stone reminds me that one day there will be a funeral for Don Piper just as there will be for every one of us.

If we can think about that stone with our name on it—whether chiseled now or one that will be in the future—it's a reminder for us to make our lives count.

I can honestly say to people, "Even if you've had a setback, or life has disappointed you, or you're in great physical pain right now, you're preparing for that final day when someone will carve a stone for you." I don't mean to be morbid or to frighten anyone. But we need a heavenly attitude—a reminder that our body might lie below the tombstone, but we'll be in heaven in the presence of a loving God.

Although I remembered the stone, my life didn't change for another twenty-five years—change in the sense of having an eternal perspective. Once we have that perspective, we not only see life differently, but we treat others differently.

Before I crossed that bridge, I ministered to needy people. I was a professional, but I also cared. But then everything changed. I still do many of the same things, but I do them from a different perspective. Or as a friend says, "Your actions now come from a different part of you." I still help, listen, visit hospitals, tell people about Jesus, preach, teach—all the things I did before. I answered the emergency calls in the middle of the night before. I still get up to rush to the ER or to talk to the parents who beg, "Can you come over? Our son is in jail."

I did those things before the accident; I do them today. But when I do those things today, I know—I truly do—that I'm doing them for God and I have the opportunity to help others change their lives.

My goal is to live each day as if it's the last day I'll spend on this earth. That doesn't mean I don't make plans, but I want to live so that I won't need tomorrow to correct the mistakes of today. I want more meaning out of each thing I do or say. I want to help others make life meaningful now.

I think it's a lot like playing the childhood game of tag. I don't see it played much today, but there was someone called It who chased another child. As soon as It tagged the other child, that child became It.

I like to think of my faith that way. I play tag often and I want every person I touch (or encounter) to feel "I'm it." I want my witness to be so strong that people can recognize that I'm the one who tags and it is my hope that once I've tagged them, they will reach out to others in the same way.

Another way to say it is that I want to leave a spiritual legacy. My legacy will be the people I've tagged and the lives I've influenced.

Having a heavenly or eternal perspective is about living in God's plan for you so you can experience a piece of heaven here and make your way to the glorious Kingdom that awaits you.

Since the release of *90 Minutes in Heaven,* I have received numerous testimonies about people who read the book just before they died. Several have read it even though they didn't know their deaths were imminent. Their families tell me that they found the book near the deathbed of one who had just gone to be with the Lord. Often people purchase the book when they sense that their time on earth is running out. I have received messages from their surviving loved ones saying how much it meant to them to read a description of heaven before going there.

Others have used excerpts from the book to comfort mourners at funeral services. Funeral homes and Christian counselors have purchased the book in quantity and given it away as a resource to encourage and comfort others. I have thought often about these responses to my experience. It is humbling to think that my experience in heaven can bring comfort to those who remain on earth or even to those who are about to leave this earth. Living our brief journey on earth with a heavenly perspective can lead to a more abundant life here and now, and an eternal life when Jesus calls us home.

In this book I've used the image of the bridge often. I still think about that bridge over Lake Livingston. I've been back to that place many times. I've parked my car and paced off the section of the bridge where the accident took place. Whenever I do that, I'm reminded of the transition I made that day, not just going to heaven and returning—but the transition to a new style of life, the transition to a heavenly perspective.

For my life to take on a heavenly perspective I had to have a car wreck. Some people have wrecked marriages, the loss of their homes, the death of spouses. Whatever the wrecks we have, to get the maximum benefit, we need the heavenly perspective.

Here's why we can have such a perspective: Heaven is real. It is the most real place I've ever been. I staked my life on the reality of heaven and my ninety minutes there proved that I had made the correct choice. I believed in heaven before I experienced it. Now that I've experienced heaven, everything has changed in my life. It's not that I doubted before—it was more a matter of focus. I'd been taught about heaven, but I hadn't thought much about it.

Now I have that heavenly perspective that influences everything I do. People don't have to die and go to heaven or even have an NDE, but they do have to realize that what we experience here now, in this life, is only preparation for what lies ahead.

TWELVE

Not the Life
I Would Have Chosen

What happens when we cross symbolic bridges?

We've all crossed many literal bridges. As soon as we exit the ramp of an actual bridge, we know we've crossed it. The Centennial Bridge across the Mississippi River takes us from Iowa to Illinois and the George Washington Bridge takes us from New Jersey to New York. We read the signs, we see the traffic from the other direction.

It's different with symbolic crossings. For one thing, we're often not aware that we've even started across the bridge. Many times we know only in retrospect. At the time we seem ignorant. As we start across, we're scarcely aware of those who have crossed those bridges before we did.

But one thing we have to realize: Our life is different once we cross that bridge—but it's not the life we have chosen; it's the one that has been chosen for us.

Before I went to heaven, I didn't think much about the place called heaven. I believed in the reality of heaven because the Bible teaches it. But I was too busy living my life to think about what would probably happen when I was eighty or ninety.

I didn't know I would cross a bridge at age thirty-eight. After that, heaven became a powerful reality. It may sound trite, but since that time I've judged my life and my activities in light of eternity. Things that once seemed of great importance no longer pull me as they once did. I don't have to race through the next intersection on yellow. I don't have to have the latest fashion in neckties, gadgets, or cars.

I'm far from alone in having a life-changing experience. Here's a story from Pamela Shively from Peru, Indiana:

"I was in a head-on crash on May 30, 1992. We never forget those dates, do we? Or even the time of day (8:30 P.M.). We were in a minivan that folded up like a pop can. I still can't bring myself to ride in one of those even after all this time. That night I drove, my husband, Steve, sat in the passenger seat, and our three children were all belted and in the back. Steve and I were not wearing our seat belts although it may have made no difference for me; possibly it would have protected Steve a little.

"The two older kids had black eyes and bruising, but they were okay. Even after several plastic surgeries, our youngest daughter, now age twenty-two, still has scars on her face. My husband rearranged his face a little on the windshield, but did not go through. He had broken ribs and a lot of bruises, but he was okay and very lucky. I had a shattered left arm, broken ribs, skull fracture, and my left leg was crushed from the knee up to the hip. My right leg was also broken.

"I spent the next two years in a wheelchair, along with fourteen surgeries (so far). My left leg was so bad they could not use the Ilizarov device you mentioned in *90 Minutes in Heaven*. I begged them to use it but, because it took so long for the bones to start healing, they feared using anything to slow that process further. My left leg is one and a half inches shorter than the right, so in that way I am fairly lucky, although that leg difference has caused pain throughout my back and right leg—which you obviously know all about.

"I was thirty-four years old at the time of the car crash. I am now forty-eight. I try always to look for the positive in our situation, but some days when my pain pills aren't working on the pain I still have, I get discouraged. I continue with physical therapy. I also go to a pain clinic and they have me on strong meds. I don't like having to do that, but as I get older, the pain and arthritic condition worsens. Most days I now walk with a cane.

"Like you, Don, I spent time in the ICU, then in the hospital, and later went to a nursing home. I came home to a hospital bed set up in my house where I lay for the next year before I could get myself in and out of bed. It was eight months before I could bathe myself. It was uplifting for me to read that someone out there actually knows how I felt, not only then but now. I still fight depression even after all these years.

"I had been very active before the car crash. I rode and showed horses professionally and hiked five miles daily until that moment. *And as you know, it changed everything within a split second.*"

Pamela said it exactly right: Everything changed in a split second. Yes, life changes and we all know that. For some, the change is slower, but it comes for all of us. And for some the bridge is one of pain every day they live. I know because I crossed the bridge and I now live the new normal.

It's not a life I would have chosen, but it is the life I have.

It is my hope that Pamela finds her new normal and is able to climb out of her depression to find the gift in her experience. I'm not trying to downplay her suffering—I've been through too much of the same to make light of it. However I know that God is with Pamela and provides a purpose out of the pain. Perhaps it's to consciously spend more time with her children, teaching them to savor the life the Lord has given them. Maybe there is a new way she can use her talent of working with animals. Her life may be different than it was before the accident, but she still has a life to live in her new normal.

Today as I drove along, the bumper sticker on the Chevy in front of me read, "Life Happens." I smiled and wondered how many times I had read that or similar statements. Today, however, I stared at those two words. I couldn't get them out of my mind. Yes, I said to myself, life does happen. For all of us, we have those times when the "happens" drastically changes everything. We can never go back to the old way—the normal behavior or circumstances.

What had been normal now becomes simply the past. Because we can't go backward, the best we can do is to learn to accept our life as it is now, move forward, and discover a new kind of normal.

Everyone's life doesn't alter as drastically as mine did, but all of us have those times when we look at *what was* and compare it with *what is*. Some of us cross symbolic bridges a number of times; others have a single experience that is as powerful a line of demarcation as the time line between B.C. and A.D. Sometimes we have to just accept the fact that this isn't the life we have chosen, but God made the choice for us. Because God made the choice for us, that means God wants to bless and enrich this phase of our lives.

It's not easy to accept and to establish the new normal. As I was to learn, I could never be the old Don Piper again. Not only had my time in heaven changed me—and that would have been enough—but my physical condition was different. Over the next fifteen years, I underwent thirty-four surgeries. Many physical activities I had taken for granted were no longer possible. My life had been transformed into a different pattern.

I want to point out three distinct things to bear in mind when we cross the Old Normal Bridge. First, we are changed in such a way that we can never unchange ourselves. It's like the action of Adam and Eve after they ate the forbidden fruit. Their eyes were opened (as the Bible puts it) and they could never regain their innocence.

My experience in dying and returning to life changed me. No matter how I looked at life after that, my perspective had been transformed. Because of my circumstances, I was able to see life from an eternal perspective. For example, many things that had seemed extremely important then, seem irrelevant now.

The second thing was that I became a physical wreck when I took the Old Normal Bridge and ended up in New Normal City. Once I was back on earth, I survived, but there were many days when I wished I hadn't. I've learned to live with a number of physical limitations. For months, I had to depend on others to do everything for me. My family was always there and friends, church members, and sometimes strangers helped my family to help me. It wasn't easy for me to admit my need.

Our tendency is to think that because we now have more limitations on our bodies, we have just as many limitations on our lives. That's not so. In fact, maybe it works the other way. The more we're aware of our physical limitations, the more we're aware of what we can't do *and* what we can do.

I never thought about physical health until I didn't have good health. Sometimes we can only see the good when we have to face the bad. God has all kinds of ways of opening our hearts and changing us. I think of the apostle Paul's entry into the Christian faith. He was present at the stoning of Stephen, the first martyr recorded in the New Testament. He didn't participate in the death itself. He just held the extra clothes of those who did.

We're never told for sure, but I believe, and so do many, that as he watched the radiant witness of Stephen, a change began to take place inside his heart. His task had been to put a stop to Christianity and do whatever necessary to make Christians recant. Then he faced a real Christian.

Here's the final statement the Bible makes about Stephen: "And as they stoned him, Stephen prayed, 'Lord Jesus, receive my spirit.' He fell to his knees, shouting, 'Lord, don't charge them with this sin!' And with that, he died" (Acts 7:59–60**).

Third, when we leave the old normal, our attitudes change; our values alter. We see people and events differently. If we've learned well, we're stronger, wiser, and more mature in relationships. If we don't learn well, we keep repeating old forms of thinking and behavior in an attempt to undo or relive the past.

Probably the most significant thing for me is that I learned to be more open with people and more aware of my own needs. I didn't have to be perfect or superhuman; I only had to learn who I was and who I was becoming.

On those three levels, my life had irrevocably altered. My old ways were just that—old ways. One of my great tasks was to figure out the new ways to live and face the world.

Obviously other people don't have the same story I have, but most of us go through one or several life-shattering experiences. They may be glorious, joyful, and positive, like my time in heaven; they may be painful, traumatic, and negative, like the 105 days I spent in a hospital after my accident.

We may have gotten married, had our first baby, landed our dream job, or inherited a large amount of money. Those changes normally reflect a joyous movement to a new normal. Life may not be quite as blessed as the dreams we have before entering into those relationships, but they're still good. As I pointed out in another place, I decided to focus on what I might call the downer changes. Not many people need encouragement to enjoy being happy. The problem is that they sometimes convince themselves that they'll be happy forever if they only get that dream job, get married, have a baby, or move to Phoenix. Life won't ever be perfect—that's reserved for heaven.

I think of the painful times that strike all of us, especially when we struggle with dreams that have failed. Some have gone through a divorce, been downsized, rejected by a parent or a child, fallen prey to an addiction, had to deal with debilitating illness, or lost a loved one. No matter what the situation, we are no longer the same individuals we were before that moment of awareness.

"What do I do now?" we ask ourselves.

Perhaps we ask our friends, "How do I get on with my life?"

One thing has to be totally clear before we can adjust and move into a new normal: We must be convinced that we can *never* go back to the way life used to be. We may struggle, cry, pray, or yearn just to have life the way it was, but we can't.

Too often most of us have heard people in the midst of their pain cry out, "I just want my life to be the way it used to be."

That won't happen.

There is no going back.

We have to adjust. We have to find a new normal.

After reading *90 Minutes in Heaven*, Anita Freeman e-mailed me:

"My husband started a new job two months ago after having searched for more than two years. For months, he tried to find something local, but he's in a technical field and there just weren't opportunities around here for him. Finally, to stay in his chosen field, he had to accept a job that is a seven-hour drive each way.

"This has placed a hardship on our family because he can come home only on weekends. Our three children seemed to adjust to his absence but it seemed too heavy a burden for me to bear. Whenever Ed left, I fell apart. I had leaned on his wisdom and strength so much. As he drove away, I went into convulsive crying because I felt totally alone. The one thing I did right was that I never let Ed see my tears. I was able to hold them until his car was gone.

"I shared my problem with two friends in a Bible study. One of them understood because her husband travels four to five days a week. That has helped and her friendship has encouraged me.

"I wanted to be able to accept Ed's absences for I knew he truly likes what he's doing. But I've been sad and even depressed. Despite his having a good job, I wanted him home with me. I have no idea how many times I cried out, 'God, I want him home. I want our life to be the way it used to be.'

"One day, I read in your book *Daily Devotions Inspired by 90 Minutes in Heaven* about the new normal. I felt as if God spoke to me right there through those words. I cried for about an hour, but your words were exactly what I needed. I had wanted our life together to be the way it had been before. Your book helped me to realize that it can't be like it was. Ed thinks that in a year or so, he may not have to travel so much. I hope that's what happens."

She thanked me for writing about the new normal and concluded, "In the meantime, while I wait for things to change, I have learned to live with *my* new normal. Not only do I find God's comfort, but I want to use my experience to comfort others."

That's the message of this book: I want to help others find the way, regain their balance, and learn to enjoy their new normal to the fullest—even after their life has drastically and unalterably changed.

Anita understood—even though it was a painful experience: Life never stays constant. Every serious change means we must leave old ways behind and accept new paths (a new normal).

We have crossed another bridge and the symbolism is that we leave something and we go on to something else. Even when we know we're going in the right direction, the adjustment is uncomfortable, and usually difficult.

But it's not impossible.

THIRTEEN

Identify and Apply the New Normal

A woman from Pennsylvania wrote to say she had undergone thirty-eight surgeries. "I'm in the middle of what you went through and the fact that you went through it encourages me to get through it. Because of your experience, I know I can make it. You were willing to let God use you in a way that showed people his love and power and strength, and that encourages people."

I appreciated her letter very much, but what she may not have realized—and many don't—is that when we are going through those terrible times our objective isn't to be a witness of God's power. Our objective at that time is simply to recover—just to find a new normal in our own lives.

I hope I can make this clear: God uses our efforts, and whatever we do that witnesses to him is something God uses. But we don't struggle through the recovery from pain to witness. We struggle through our pain to survive. During our worst times, our immediate goal is to make it.

All through my long ordeal I would have laughed if anyone had talked to me about the power of my witness. The power of the witness is something that comes later. It comes as part of the survival, but also from some of the learning.

I think of a friend in Idaho who went through a terrible period of a broken marriage and the loss of his lucrative job almost simultaneously. Two years later, he said, "I'm paying my bills; my former wife has taken all our assets, and I could probably grumble about a lot of things, but I'm all right. I've learned so much about myself in the process." He went on to say he had thought about the term *new normal* and "It's a good tag for where I am now. I don't know where my life will go, but I know I like myself a lot better."

I remember talking to him when he was in the midst of his struggle. A month after his marriage broke up, he cried on the phone and kept saying, "I just don't think I can make it. I don't see any light out of this dark, dark tunnel." After he cried, he asked, "Is it worth holding on?"

He has seen the light and he's now walking in it.

A man called me to seek counsel as he and his wife went through a difficult period in their marriage. They wanted children, but were unable to have them. The wife had conceived twice and had been unable to carry the babies to full term. I understood that. Between the birth of our twins and the birth of our daughter, Nicole, Eva lost two. It's an extraordinarily painful situation for most people, especially if they truly want children.

I listened to him for a long time. He needed to talk about their pain. "I don't have an answer for you," I said. "We don't understand many things in this life. But I do know that if you truly want children, and you feel in your heart that you are called to parent, there are options for you to explore. You first have to accept the reality of your situation—your wife may never be able to carry a baby to term—but from that point you can move forward and figure out how to live in your new reality."

This couple eventually decided to adopt and have now adopted two children. She told my wife, "When I read your husband's book I thought it was fascinating, but you know what has happened? As a result of reading that book I decided I would become the best mother to my adopted children that I can possibly be. I've decided that will be my new normal." She briefly mentioned how hard they had tried to have their natural children and the pain they went through. "I'm going to focus on not what I couldn't do, which is to be the biological mother of children, but I'm going to focus on what I can do and that is be the best mother to these two adopted children that I could ever possibly be."

I loved it when Eva told me that story. It says to me that there are no limits to the things people go through and the struggles they have until they learn to accept and apply the new normal.

I spoke with another couple who had a similar situation and the husband summed up their attitude this way: "A lot of people have babies and don't really want them. We couldn't have biological children but we have three special children—children that God sent to us. We're so blessed to be able to raise three children who otherwise might not know what a loving home can be."

That's the new normal and they love their new way of life. But I couldn't have told them that three years ago. In those days, adoption wasn't a word they wanted to hear. They would have thought of adoption as some kind of substitute for the real thing. They were still trying fertility clinics and reading everything they could on the Internet. Now they're at peace. They decided to celebrate and frequently tell their children how blessed they are. "God gave us to you and gave you to us."

Their new normal is to focus on what they can do. And in the focus to give thanks to God.

When people are injured in accidents, everything transpires in an instant. They're fully alive one moment and then life turns upside down. They never know what will happen the next moment—or if there will be a next. Tomorrow *is* another day, but we don't know if we'll survive to see tomorrow. The next hour is a new hour, but we might not have another hour. Under normal circumstances, none of us expects to die today or this week, but it happens.

I want to tell you one of the things that ended up having much more of an impact than I thought it would. Eva has a friend who didn't want to go through physical therapy after an accident. She knew, and so did her family, that it would be an extremely slow and very painful process.

I understood and could still vividly remember when the doctors made me do things that hurt—just plain hurt. They forced me to do things I didn't want to do. I told Eva's friend several of the terrible ordeals I went through. I told her I did those things, but not with any joy or sense of accomplishment. But people observed me and saw something I didn't know at the time. While I saw my weaknesses—what I couldn't do—they saw my strength.

They witnessed my perseverance, and even if I could only walk one step before I fell, they saw that it was one more step than I could take the day before.

Eva's friend heard my words and witnessed what I can do now and made the decision to undergo the therapy. She wouldn't focus on how painful it would be or how long it would take. She would simply take it one day at a time and celebrate every step God enabled her to take.

It reminded me of a poem I read years ago by Dietrich Bonhoeffer, a young theologian of great promise, who was martyred by the Nazis for his participation in a plot against the life of Adolf Hitler shortly before the end of World War II. The poem is called, "Who Am I?" The guards regarded him as cheerful and courageous, but on the inside he felt unsure and weak. He struggled over who he really was, but at the end he came to one conclusion: Whoever he was, God knew, and Bonhoeffer knew he belonged to God.

My point is that we hardly know who we are and we have no idea how our lives touch others. I'm still amazed at the people who praise my story of endurance and tell me how greatly I inspire them. People have watched me and my life, and my heaven story has had a great deal of meaning to them.

For some people, I am a powerful witness; to Don Piper, I'm a guy who struggles each day but who knows the last bridge to cross is still ahead. I'm hobbling toward that final bridge and I've chosen to enjoy the view along the way.

Perhaps I'm wrong, but I think many people respond to me as they do because they need encouragement and seek some kind of model that says, "You can do this." For many their question is, "Can I make it through this current trauma?"

The one thing I can genuinely offer is hope. Here's what I wish everyone would hear: No matter how bad things look or how devastated you may feel, you are not alone, and you are never alone. God is with you—even if you're not aware of his presence.

In this book, I write a lot about the new normal. I do that because it has been one of the most powerful concepts of my life since God gave it back to me.

When people talk to me about the new normal, here's the only caution I offer: Your new normal may not be what you think it will be or should be. You will likely end up at a different place than where you thought. In fact, it's almost a guarantee because none of us can perceive what the new normal will be.

For me, the big objective in my new normal was to walk again. I did that (finally) and people are still amazed, *but I did it.* But there are always surprises. The new normal can be burdensome. At times, I feel an obligation to be mobile and walk even better. I do the best I can, but my legs aren't the same legs they were before the accident.

For example, I flew into Atlanta to work with Cec Murphey on this book. When I got back to my room after dinner, my legs hurt. I sat on the couch and took off my shoes. I stared down and I couldn't find my ankles. I took off my socks and my pants and saw that both legs were incredibly swollen. I couldn't see any veins in my feet.

I tell this because we can't assume the new normal means we'll be as good as new in our bodies, in our businesses, or in our personal relationships. It does mean we'll be different.

Part of entering into the new normal is to set goals for the past, the present, and the future. First, our goal is to release the past. We can't relive it and it's over. Someone said to me, it doesn't matter whether you're someone who lingers over the past or dashes through it, the old party is over and we can't attend it again.

Second is to set goals for the present. If we could live with the old normal, we would never need a new normal. Instead this is our time of new beginnings. We can make changes and we can learn to adapt. It's the ending that makes the new normal possible. I've also learned something: Most of our important beginnings take place in the darkness—that is, outside our awareness. I write about the darkness because that's an important aspect of the new normal. We haven't truly embraced the new normal until we've been through the dark places. My theory is that the most powerful learning takes place when we're totally unconscious of it. Sometimes we just move from day to day. We can't even think of the future, only of taking the next step.

I've heard the stories of utter devastation. There are people who have been maimed, blinded in an accident, lost a mate or a child, had their homes burned and lost everything they owned. Those are terrible things. But once they have moved into a new normal they say that they were so busy trying to survive, they didn't realize the techniques they had learned or the survival skills they had employed. "I just wanted to get through it," they said.

But once they are able to live in the present, they need to think about their aims and desires for present-time living. "Here's what I want to do now that I've moved into the new normal," and they can set those present, foreseeable goals:

- I want to adopt a child.
- I want to start a new career.

• I want to get more training so I can have a better job.
• I want to share my story and encourage others.

One man blinded in an accident told me the long story of his life and all the things he couldn't do. He grieved over that for months, but one day, he heard himself say, "Okay, now I need to figure out what I can do." That's what I mean by the present goal setting.

No matter what our aspirations, we need also to be open to God to change them. I planned to go back to being a pastor. I couldn't work with youth anymore so I began to work with educational programs and seniors. No matter what we plan, God might make it even better.

I didn't plan to write books about my experiences. Even after I contracted for my first book, I had no idea that I'd be asked to speak across the United States and other parts of the world.

The enormous sale of my books and the speaking engagements came as a result of my goal setting for the present—to figure out what I could do now. To my total surprise, my tragic and difficult accident has not only touched people but my new normal has increased so that I'm able to minister to larger groups and in more places. It's more than just the opportunity to hold their hands and say, "I'm so sorry." Today when I hear stories of pain and struggle, I understand—I truly do—and they know I understand.

That became part of my new normal. I never planned for that. My plan was to walk with my own two feet, to encourage others who were going through physical pain, and to share what little I knew. To talk about the reality of heaven was never part of my plan. If my good friend David Gentiles had not said, "You have to tell people," I probably would still have kept it secret.

Third, we need to look toward the future. God always seems to have bigger plans for us than we have for ourselves. We think small; God thinks big. Although he's interested in the most minute details, he has a big-picture scheme and knows where our lives are headed. That's exciting.

That awareness takes the responsibility off me. I do the best I can for God's glory but I don't have to worry about where it's all going. That's one of the great blessings about my journey to heaven. I know where it will end because God has a sovereign plan at work.

Here's something else that has helped me to apply the new normal: the response of others. I can hardly begin to relate how others have blessed me. God has taken my broken body and given me enough strength to reach out, and people have responded beyond anything I would have imagined. They share their hurts, their confidences, and give me their trust. That's humbling. That's also God at work.

FOURTEEN

Why Me?

Helena,[3] a reader I'd never met, e-mailed me in late 2006 and marveled at my story about heaven.

"At the store, *90 Minutes in Heaven* caught my eye. I snatched it up, took it home to read, and I couldn't put it down until I had finished it. I was so touched by the words I read. I read your vivid descriptions of heaven. I can picture in some small way what it will be like. You will never know how much you helped me. I was at the end of myself and so depressed I just wanted to die. Eleven months ago, my husband of four weeks had a sudden heart attack and died in my arms. Since the age of ten he knew he wanted to be a minister of the gospel and planned his life that way. He graduated from seminary eight days before we married and had been called as a pastor to a rural church in Arkansas. He died one week before he was to preach his first sermon as pastor.

[3] At her request, I have changed the names and location.

"'Why, God, why?' I screamed that night and hundreds of other times. 'If you had to take him, why did you do it now? Why not after a year or five years? Why did you take him before he had a chance to serve you as a pastor?' For almost a year I cried out, 'God? Why are you picking on me?'

"After I finished reading your book, I realized you've gone through far worse things than I have and you've come through victoriously. I still don't know why such terrible things happen and why Ronald (my husband) died, but I have the assurance that he's inside heaven's gate right now and filled with joy and rejoicing. I wish I could put into words how your life and ministry have eased the pain in my heart.

"Since I became a believer at age nine, I've known that I would go to heaven but I never thought much about it. For me, heaven was where eighty-year-old people went. Ronald went fifty years early; he was only thirty.

"I read your description of heaven five times before the tears began to fall. I don't know how long I wept, but it must have been for at least an hour. I realized that I was angry with God, and even angry at Ronald for dying. I suppose that may sound silly, but I was. 'Why did you leave me? Why did you do this to me?' I screamed, and it sounds a little crazy to write that.

"Your story has given me peace. Because you've been to heaven and come back to share that experience, I am ready to move on with my life. I know Ronald can't hear me, but if he could, I'd tell him that it's all right that he left me.

"Yes, Mr. Piper, heaven is real. I've known it more as a kind of intellectual statement of faith, but you've helped me to see it as a real place and I have a reserved room."

Here's another e-mail I received from Jessica Smith:

"After reading your story, I just felt that I had to write to you, tell you some things that have gone on in my life recently, and thank you for restoring my faith. My family owns Quantum Leap Skydiving, and my older brothers, Jim and Scott Cowan, operated it. On July 29, 2006, the Otter [plane] crashed, instantly killing my brother Scott and five other wonderful people. My brother was the pilot and had been a pilot for many years. I was hurt, devastated, confused, and angry. I kept asking myself, why would God take my brother like that? Why now? Those questions led to more questions and to few answers and a lot of anger. I kept wondering where he was, and if heaven was real.

"Thank you for making heaven a reality to me."

Jessica wrote us again just before the publication of this book: "I thought I would give you an update on my last letter. The last time that I wrote to you, my mom was in the hospital with metastatic breast cancer. She passed away on November 11. Right before she died, she smiled in relief for being free from pain, misery, and fear, and actually opened her eyes for the first time in days.

"We asked if Scotty (my brother who was killed in the plane crash) was coming to get her and she nodded. That was the end.

"I just know heaven is real, and it made me think of your experience when you said you had been surrounded by the people that you loved. I've been traumatized that I'm only nineteen and yet I've lost my mom and brother three months apart, but I'm relieved to know that she's happy now and in heaven. Thank you so much for your inspiration, hope, and faith."

I could give many illustrations that have come to me through e-mails, phone calls, and one-on-one conversations that started with a question that people were unable to get past for a long time. It's a question most of us ask at some point or another. That question is: Why is this happening to me?

First comes the question, "Why me?" Right behind that is often a second question: "Why now?"

I can't begin to explain why or why now. Even if I could, I don't think people really want the answers. I think they ask the questions because they feel isolated or abandoned.

I can, however, offer suggestions to people who are going through painful transitions in their lives.

First, we need to take care of ourselves. This isn't the time to focus on being your highest, to ask how you can be a better person or a stronger Christian. It's okay to be weak and vulnerable. Instead, look at your own needs and don't force yourself to change as if you had to swallow bitter medicine. When I lay for months in the hospital, I had enough sense not to focus on the big issues of life. I just wanted to endure another day—to get past the pain of that day. I struggled with depression and the uselessness of my life (at the time I thought it was useless). But I did learn to take care of myself and to allow others to help me.

Second, we need to explore the other side of the bridge. Some changes are the result of our own actions; others aren't. If we choose the bridge, we may regret or ask ourselves why we did it, but we know it was our decision.

There are times our bridges are not of our own choosing: when a company downsizes, a loved one dies, a relationship ends. We don't understand why this has happened to us and we tend not to see the benefits. We're so caught up in the misery of the present, we can't see ahead. That's natural and normal.

I must be honest: I never saw the vast ministry that God had in mind for me. For a long time I tried to make the best of my life after I crossed the car-crash bridge. It took two years to talk about heaven and *fifteen years* before I was able to see the practical benefit of my trip to heaven. I'm not sure anyone could have helped me explore that other side. I would have thought they were unrealistic.

Third, we need to find someone to talk to—someone who cares and understands. Whether you choose a professional counselor or a good friend, you need a listening ear. It wasn't easy for me to do that. I needed people like my wife, Eva, or my friends David Gentiles, Cliff McArdle, Jay B. Perkins, Todd Lochner, and Matt Mealer.

What I learned was that I didn't need a lot of advice—and most of us don't. What I needed was to put into words my feelings and my dilemma so that another person could hear, reflect, and show compassion. I didn't need someone to give me easy answers (or even hard ones), but someone to accept me as I was and at my worst, and still care.

My cowriter, Cecil Murphey, defines a true friend as "someone who knows all about you, still loves you, and has no plan for your self-improvement." Those are the kind of people we need to hear us.

Fourth, we need to step out and away from the bridge. We need to discover what's on the other side and beyond our present experience. When I opened up to David Gentiles and told him about my heavenly trip, he all but demanded that I speak and tell people. He urged me not to hold on to the experience as if it were only mine. I was hesitant to share my story, but I would never have developed a worldwide ministry if I hadn't stepped out and begun to talk about my experience.

Mindy Poole wrote that her friend and coworker, Laurie, let her borrow my book on CD. "She and I have listened to it and talked about what a difference it has made in our lives as far as witnessing and about heaven. We are both Christians and speak often of our spiritual walks.

"I told my dad and my father-in-law about your book and talked about what an impact it had on us, when my phone rang. Laurie's sixteen-year-old son had just died in an automobile accident. I was shocked and devastated.

"She called me the night of the accident and the first thing she said was that she was so happy that she read your book. It comforted her in her pain, knowing what Logan was seeing and feeling and hearing.

"It was no coincidence that we both read your book. God prepared us for this event in her life. Thank you for telling your story so that we as Christians can continue to encourage each other in our race for the finish."

Laurie was able to step away from the bridge and see beyond her present pain. That was a powerful step in her moving ahead.

Many husbands die before their wives and we have many widows in the world. I talk to them regularly and the question I hear most often from them is the why question.

"Why did God leave me here alone? I'm the survivor. Why didn't He take me and leave him?"

Again, I have no answers, but I want to share a story that I heard years ago. A preacher spoke about the death of his mother. His parents had been married for more than fifty years. The son flew home for the funeral and he was surprised at how calm and peaceful his father was. On the day of the funeral, the father said little. He greeted the people who came to the funeral and expressed his appreciation for their remembering his late wife.

Afterward the pastor and his father went back to the house. Late in the afternoon, they sat on rocking chairs on the front porch to watch the evening skies darken. For perhaps an hour not a word passed between them.

The father stopped rocking and said, "I want to go back out to the cemetery."

The pastor-son objected. "The sun's going down. By the time we get out to the cemetery it'll be dark. They don't have any lights out there."

"That's all right. I still want to go."

The son didn't understand but he agreed to take his father. They got in the pickup and drove to the cemetery. By then it was totally dark with heavy clouds and only a sliver of a moon. The son parked so that the headlights showed them the gravesite.

They got out of the vehicle and walked in silence to the grave. They were so isolated, they could hear no sounds other than the crunch of their shoes as they walked across the grassy lots.

The father stared silently at the grave. Several minutes passed before the old man said, "This is the way it should be."

"I'm sorry, Dad, I don't understand."

"She should go first."

"I don't understand," the son said.

"She should go first. Now she doesn't have to feel like I do now."

All of us lose people we love. I constantly talk to people who have lost those they love. Most of us know what it's like. It hurts and the pain doesn't evaporate or go away overnight. But the survivors remain. If we believe in a sovereign God, we also know we have stayed behind for a reason.

We may never grasp the reason—and we may not need to know the reason—but we do need to get past the mourning stage. When we lose someone, it's grief about ourselves: It's *our* loss. It's *our* pain.

I think it's good to take whatever time we need to feel our loss. Scream if we need to, cry if it helps. We need to be kind to ourselves and comfort ourselves with good memories of the past. We may need to remind ourselves of the presence of God in our lives to strengthen us during those times.

Many tell me that after they have moved beyond the why question after the loss of a loved one, they can focus ahead. They have crossed a bridge and want to live the final portion of their lives as well as they can.

"I know the separation is only temporary," one woman said to me. "Heaven is real and because I know that, I can enjoy now as I look ahead."

FIFTEEN

Only One Life

"Why can't I just off myself?" the young man asked. "I'm in pain all the time and I'll never walk." That was one of the first times anyone had talked seriously to me about suicide. He was in a wheelchair and came to a book signing.

"You can take your own life," I said, "but I hope you won't."

I waited for him to speak and he opened up. Within fifteen minutes I heard about a really bad life. Much of his trouble came because of his parents' bad choices about drugs and alcohol. But he had also made bad choices about drugs, sex, and risky living. He told me that he sat in the wheelchair because of an attempted suicide. He had raced his car down the highway with his foot pressed tightly against the accelerator. He closed his eyes as his car picked up speed.

His car hit an embankment, flipped over four times, and threw him to the side of the road. Aside from broken limbs, he was paralyzed from the waist down.

"I hate my life," he said. "I hate it every day."

I didn't say anything because I wasn't sure what to say, so I just waited.

"Give me a reason to live. Just one."

"Because you want to live." The words just came to me. Then I said, "You wouldn't ask the question if you wanted to die." I went on to tell him that he had only one life, but that life doesn't end at the grave. "That's only the transition." I pointed out that the Bible tells us clearly that life is eternal. We get to choose if we want to live in God's presence or in the place of eternal torment.

"I have to know one thing," he said and his pale blue eyes stared intently at me. "Just one thing. Please, please don't lie to me."

"I'll answer any question you ask."

He held up a copy of *90 Minutes in Heaven*. "Is heaven real? I mean did you truly go there or did you just go into some kind of trance or coma or—?"

I put my hand on his shoulder and didn't turn away my gaze. "It's the most real thing in the world. Because it's real, I'm here today in this bookstore. I'm here to offer hope."

Tears streaked down his face. "I'm miserable and I make everyone else miserable."

"You can change," I said. "You can call on God, who will strengthen you and help you change."

I don't know the end of his story, but we prayed together. He promised me that he would talk with a local pastor. I hope he did.

His is a sad story and I encounter many of them. I talk to parents and siblings of those who have taken their lives. They also suffer and often blame themselves for the death of that loved one.

Some people are more naturally equipped to deal with life's exigencies and ongoing problems. For some, they can think only of escape right now. Tomorrow or the day after doesn't enter their thoughts.

Others carry on but they've reached the point of hopelessness and despondency so deep and intense that they don't want to see the sun come up in the morning. They don't want to talk to anybody. They wrap themselves in a cocoon of isolation. I meet people like that regularly.

Others aren't quiet. They're bitter and angry because of the circumstances in their lives. Their rage prevents them from living a full life. For example, before the service began at a church in Arkansas, I spoke with a middle-aged woman whose friends had brought her with them. Her son had died in an automobile accident that wasn't his fault. Someone else ran into him and had taken his life.

She let me know that she came with reluctance. The anger was written all over her body. I particularly noticed the tenseness of her jaws. She cried a lot, but they were bitter tears.

"They brought me to hear you and I've come because they insisted and wouldn't give up. So I'm here. I don't like it, but I'm here."

"I'm glad you came anyway—"

"I'm here, but I don't know what good it will do me. I'm upset. I don't know why God took my son." She spoke of suicide and that life had no meaning. The words erupted and I listened until someone pulled on my sleeve. "It's time for the service to begin."

As I walked away, I thought about that bitter woman and prayed silently that God would help her and give her peace. I preached a sermon about heaven, in which I described heaven and how to get there. The church bulletin titled it "The Cure for Heart Trouble." I talked about heaven in all its detail as vividly as

I could. Sometimes people feel frustrated that I don't say more about it, but I say what I know and stop. I don't speculate on what I didn't see or don't know.

A few people have complained, "You just gave me a taste of heaven; I want more."

"So do I," I usually say. "But like you, I have to wait to get it all." I also tell them that if I said more, I'd be making it up.

I finished the service and the church had a book table in the foyer. People lined up and I autographed copies. I looked up once and saw that same angry woman near the end of the line. I wondered what she would say this time. She had been so bitter and I wondered if my sermon had angered her even more.

Her turn came and she thrust her book in front of me. Before she could say a word, the tears raced down her cheeks. I handed the book back to her and as I did, she grabbed my hand.

I stared at her and I sensed something had changed. The tightness in her jaw was gone and, despite the tears, her face glowed. "God sent me here tonight. He truly sent me here tonight."

I smiled and tried to think of something to say.

She continued, "Tonight is the beginning of changing bitter into better. I know where my son is. I hadn't thought of that before. I thought only about how much I love him and miss him—I miss him every day."

"I hope that comforts you."

"Oh it does! It does!" she cried out. "As I listened to you speak, I knew that I wouldn't want him to come back from heaven. And I've just got to help other people who have gone through the same thing to get there."

I have rarely seen such a drastic change in a person in such a brief period and I told her so.

"I need to help others to get where I am right now. That's my goal, and I want to live for that."

"I want to pray with you right now," I said, and I heard the quiver in my own voice. "I want to pray that God will give you what you need because this is just the first step. Much is going to have to happen for this to take place."

"I know it, but it is the *first* step." She told me of ideas that had already come to her and how she was determined to make her life count. "This is a new day for me. It's just a new day."

When she heard about the reality of heaven, that woman was able to leave her bitterness behind. Not everyone does; not everyone can. I don't blame them; I do pity them. I understand what it's like to be knocked down. I understand what it's like to be depressed. I understand what it's like to be hopeless. And that's where a lot of people are. But we really need to change that hopelessness into hope. And we need to change that mess into a message. We need to change that disappointment into divine appointments. And it begins with a decision. Her decision was to leave her bitterness behind.

Here's another example. A man named Rob[4] sent me an e-mail.

"I've read your book. I've had issues with a back injury for the past eight months and on one occasion, I held a loaded gun to my head." He's in the health field and wrote about his career. "I've spent the last twenty years helping other people through life and death."

He gave examples and then wrote, "I've lived a good life, and I've tried to help other people. Now look at this thing that happened to me. I find it more than coincidental that I picked up

---

[4] He doesn't wish to be identified by his real name.

your book in a grocery store during this trying time and the fact that you were injured at my exact age, that's thirty-eight. What's more, I have completely converted from an agnostic, or as I termed it, from a casual observer to a Christian. I have more faith in God now than I've ever had in my life and no fear of death, which I always have had. All I ask you is this, that you say a prayer for me. I believe you have been touched by God and your story was instrumental in converting me to a believer. If a moment of your time could be taken to pray for my recovery it would mean everything. I am once again in excruciating pain and what should have been the end of a long ordeal has taken another wrong turn."

His words touched me, especially his last paragraph: "I put down the gun once, but if I lift it again, I know it will be the last time. I just want to be out of pain and working in a hospital again. But if that is not to be, then I want to go to heaven."

Rob is in a place where no one wants to be. He daily experiences despair, hopelessness, and pain. He can't get across that bridge. He's crying on the middle of that bridge.

There are many, many out there. I talk to other Robs almost every day. I've prayed many times for that Rob and I've asked God not to let him even think of picking up the gun again.

I'm always touched that people will open up and tell me that they've thought of taking their lives with guns or pills or any other form of suicide. That fact alone says they want help.

"You've taken the first step," I say. "As soon as you tell someone you need help, you have begun the road to emotional and spiritual recovery." I applaud Rob and others who make that effort. He reached out to a stranger. He wrote to me because he read one of my books, but he doesn't know me. And yet he feels he does because he read and shared an intimate part of my life. I felt I shared a poignant moment in Rob's life. Now he needs to open up to others who can care and be with him.

I don't know what Rob will do, but if he will open up to others about his pain—on every level—he can be a marvelous resource person in the health-care industry. He can turn around his pain and use it to help others.

When I think of the turnaround of such individuals, immediately I think of the words of the great apostle Paul: "All praise to the God and Father of our Lord Jesus Christ. God is our merciful Father and the source of all comfort. He comforts us in all our troubles so that we can comfort others" (2 Corinthians 1:3–4a**).

This statement has been my personal mandate for service. I preached before my accident and I preached truth as much as I knew it. But the reality of heaven changed my preaching. Now I preach out of a heavenly experience.

As I think of Rob, I wonder what will happen. He may never be able to do what he did before. I don't know how much of his strength and health have been taken from him. But even if he feels as if he is, Rob isn't useless. God isn't finished with his life and I know God can and will open avenues of service.

I have only to look at myself. Before the accident, I was what I call a moderately successful pastor and enjoyed my life. Now I have the opportunity to touch the lives of millions. I pushed away and fought depression and suicidal thoughts—yes, I had them. I had no sense of any great mission ahead. In the beginning of my recuperation, I only wanted to live. After that, I realized I had a message to share—a message borne out of my own life.

Rob has already taken the biggest step: He has surrendered his life to God and now he's ready for service. That's all the Lord asks.

If I could talk to Rob, to the bitter, the discouraged, and the suicidal right now, here's what I would say: "You wonder why you should live? I will tell you why. You need to live to help others. The reason is simple: God has allowed you to live. Each of us remains on earth for a reason. Our purposes may not be obvious or clear, but we're not left by mistake."

I've talked to those who have lost loved ones. I've met people whose homes burned and who have lost things of value to them. But it's also refreshing that most of them finally get over that bridge of loss and despair. When they tell me their stories they say, "I thought I had lost everything, but the fire didn't destroy my family. It didn't destroy my job. It didn't destroy my friends."

Did the fire destroy some extremely important memories? Absolutely. It's a great tragedy and a horrific loss. And yet I have known people over the years who have lost everything that way and who have reconstructed their lives and have ended up becoming invaluable resources to people who are going through the same thing.

What we think of as tragedy may be a powerful transition—and a positive one. I don't want to make light of this, but no matter how terrible the situation, it is just one more bridge we have to cross on our way to the final bridge to heaven.

SIXTEEN

Using Pain

Long after I recovered from my accident I heard about Andrea, a fifteen-year-old girl who had been in a boating accident. She and her dad were on Jet Skis when they had a major collision with each other. They got tangled and Andrea caught her right leg on the broken fiberglass of her demolished Jet Ski. The accident did massive damage to her leg in terms of muscle loss, tissue loss, and broken bones. They put one of those fixators on her leg to save it—just as I had on mine.

About ten months later they removed her fixator. She started to recover well but developed a serious infection. They were afraid she would lose her leg. The staff told her father that the lake was filled with parasites and a wild array of bacteria.

In the midst of that crisis, her father called me. He said he had read my books. "I read the story, especially the one about the high school boy at the church that you went over to see."

I had an emotional encounter with a young man who had been badly injured in a skiing accident and wore an external fixator on his leg like the one I had to wear after my accident. His hopes of a football career were dashed. While everyone who encountered him offered encouragement and prayers, he could never seem to find someone who gave him hope for a meaningful life. No one had suffered what he was enduring. I had, and I was privileged to help him find hope.

"Yes, I remember that boy very well."

"I know this is being imposing, but is there any way you could pray for Andrea?"

"I'd really rather see her if that's possible. Where is she?"

"She's at Hermann Hospital."

"Excellent. I'm going down near there for an MRI tomorrow and I'll drop by to see her. It may be better if she didn't have an audience. She's more likely to open up if she doesn't have a bunch of people standing around listening to her. I should be there no later than two P.M.," I said.

The next day, a few minutes before two, I knocked on the door of her room, which was in the pediatric section. I walked inside and introduced myself. Her mother and a family friend were in the room.

"My name is Don Piper and you don't know me but I was in a bad accident a few years ago and I had a fixator."

She was shy, but she said, "Uh-huh," and nodded.

"They're awful, aren't they?"

"Yeah. Awful."

"You've got an infection—one that's pretty bad. But I want you to know that you can get over this. You can recover from this."

She turned her face away.

"I'm serious. I can tell you about this because I had one of those on my leg and had an infection."

"Really?" She looked at me.

"I was thirty-eight when my accident happened. But I want you to know that today—just now—I actually walked to Hermann Hospital from St. Luke's. Do you know where St. Luke's is?"

"No."

"It's four blocks from here. To be honest with you, if I had to do it all over again I probably wouldn't have walked, because I had forgotten how far it was. But I did walk, even though it tired me."

I paused and waited for her to respond. She didn't say anything but I knew she was listening.

"I did it. I went through a lot of pain—just as you're going through right now. But I beat the pain. I got over the infection."

She nodded slightly and I think she wanted to believe me.

"And you can, too. I walked the four blocks here, and when I leave your room, I have to walk all the way back down there because that's where my appointment is."

Now I had her interest. I reached inside my coat pocket and pulled out photos that I seldom allow anyone to see. "May I show you my pictures?" Without waiting for her to reply, I showed her. "Here's what mine looked like."

"Oh."

"It's not quite like the one you had because they've made some refinements on them. They don't use as much stainless steel. They use graphite and some other stuff, but it's still the same principle. Put the rods through, turn the screws—"

"Oh, yeah, I know."

"I want to be honest with you, Andrea. This ordeal will be extraordinarily painful. The only hope I can offer you is to give you the old saying 'This too shall pass.' And you will overcome this. Do your therapy, and obviously you'll have to take the antibiotics because you have an infection. Do whatever they tell you. Let people help you." I almost smiled as I said those words because I remembered how difficult it had been for me to let anyone help.

"I know you just want to get this over with and go on with the rest of your life. I understand that but you have to remember that everybody else wants it as much as you do. Together let's do it. I'm willing to partner with you. Here's what I want to do. If you'll cooperate and get well, one of these days I want to visit you. I want to do that so that we can take a walk together."

She stared at me as if to ask, "Are you serious?"

"I am. I would like to walk with you. That would be a goal for me: that just the two of us would go for a walk some day," I said. "You're fifteen and your prom is in a couple of years. I'll tell you what, you keep progressing, you do what you need to do, you do your therapy, do your rehabilitation and that kind of stuff. I'll come to your prom and we'll dance together. How about that?"

"That'd be nice." Despite her shyness, she smiled, and I knew she would give it her best.

"I'm going to leave in a minute but I want you to know that I just wanted to give you hope. You finally met somebody who gets what's going on and who knows what that thing feels like. I'm sure everybody has patted you on the shoulder and said, 'Oh, sweetheart, it's going to be okay, we're praying for you,' and you just want to hit them."

At that point she smiled and said, "Yeah, that's right."

"I get it. I do understand. I'll be honest with you, Andrea, I didn't confide in anybody when I went through this. There wasn't anybody—at least no one I knew—who had had one of those fixators. If they were out there I didn't know who they were. And I grant you there may not have been anybody. Mine was only the sixth femur Ilizarov installed in the country, so there really was no one to relate to."

"Really?"

"Really. It's fairly common now, as I'm sure you've been told. I'm determined that I'm going to be that person for you to relate to and that's why I came to see you today. Your dad called me and asked me to visit." I told her I had to leave for my appointment, but I added, "I want you to call me." I handed her my card with my phone number on it. "And I want to pray for you. Can you let me do that right now?"

"Oh, yes, I'll let you."

We held hands and I prayed for Andrea. I called on Jesus as the great physician to do a healing that would exceed our expectations. All the time I was aware that that healing may not be a complete healing in one sense but it might be a totally different healing in another.

After prayer, I left but I was serious then—as I am still—and I want to go to her prom and take a walk with her when she's ready. I know she will make it.

This e-mail is a follow-up to the Andrea story:

"Last April, my husband, Jeff, contacted you and you graciously visited my daughter Andrea (then fifteen years old) and me at Hermann Hospital in Houston during one of her many stays there. Infection had reoccurred in her right leg (the one on which she previously had a fixator) and she was having a hard time dealing with the prognosis. Your visit meant a great deal to me and to Andrea, too. Even though she never talked much about it, I could tell.

"Since then, Andrea has improved so much. She has had several more surgeries for infection, also for a bone graft and a plate, but her bone has grown and she is walking again. Praise God.

"You told her in the hospital that you looked forward to taking a walk with her one day and at the time, it was hard to believe. But now it is possible.

"She will need to have the plate removed (possibly this summer) because of an infection that reoccurred after she received it, but the prognosis is excellent. The Lord has also given her his encouragement over the months and her depression has lifted.

"Something happened yesterday at a routine visit to her plastic surgeon's office that I feel compelled to tell you about. As always, Dr. Melissinos's waiting room was filled with patients in wheelchairs, many of them with fixators on their legs and arms. That was the first time Andrea had been able to walk into the office without the aid of a wheelchair or crutches—an exciting milestone.

"As we waited to be called in to see the doctor, conversations went on. Several individuals told about their accidents and experiences. A woman across the room with a fixator on her leg mentioned that she had purchased a book this week that she was going to read. 'It's called *90 Minutes in Heaven*,' she said. 'It's about a pastor who had died after a car wreck, went to heaven, and returned to earth again.'

"To my amazement, Andrea spoke up and said, 'I met him. I met the man that wrote that book. He came to see me in the hospital.'

"Another woman asked her about her experience, and she told everyone in the room that she had gone through thirteen surgeries and she was finally able to walk. She encouraged a woman whose daughter was in a wheelchair and whose grand-daughter had been killed. 'Things will get better,' Andrea said.

"After she rolled up her pants leg and showed everyone her leg, she got up and walked across the room to show them how well she walked. She assured them they would get better, even though it didn't seem like it now. 'It just takes time.'

"With tears in her eyes, the woman who had bought the book came over and hugged Andrea when she left. She told our daughter how much she had encouraged her.

"Jeff and I were amazed that Andrea would speak up. In the past, she had not wanted to bring attention to her leg or the accident. A month or so ago, Jeff asked her about giving a video testimony with us for church, but she said no. Yet, in that situation, God prompted her to speak. He certainly leads in his timing.

"God continues to use your story and your visit to see her in the hospital to bring healing, not only to her, but to others. Thank you for letting the Spirit lead you that day you visited Andrea in the hospital. I will never forget it. I pray God will lead you and Andrea to meet again one day and take that walk together."

I went into detail on that story because it illustrates how we can use our pain. I wouldn't begin to try to figure out the reasons for my accident and my trip to heaven. That's all God's business. My responsibility is to ask, "What do I do now?"

What I do now—among other things—is to use the memory of my own injuries, the scars, and the ongoing pain in my body to touch other people in their pain.

What amazes me is that my problems revolve around my physical hurts and mobility. When I talk to people, some tell me about their physical problems, but they also open up about their spiritual issues. They tell me about their inner hurts. They share things with me that I sometimes wonder if they've ever told another person. I've heard stories of abortion, rape, incest, infidelity, and just about everything else.

Why do they come to me? I don't know for sure, but here are the answers that give me peace. *First, they come because they sense I care and that I understand.* I don't mean to brag or imply that I'm anything special, because I know I'm not.

What I do know is that I died and experienced the reality of heaven. Not only did God send me back to live again, but I returned with a mangled body. I don't like the pain or the limitations—I don't want to give the impression that I do. What I rejoice in is that my weaknesses and my ordeal enable me to relate to people.

I think of the couple whose child died in a swimming pool or the young woman confined to a wheelchair for life because of her drug overdose.

Many of the e-mails I receive are about those who have been gravely injured in accidents involving motorcycles. Many have suffered serious brain damage or paralysis. Others have lost children at birth or shortly afterward. Eva and I lost children between the births of Nicole and our twins, Chris and Joe. So many people experience pain and heartbreak. Such hurting people are around us all the time. We need to learn to pause and see their pain.

When I ponder why they come to me, I think I may know a second reason: *They want assurance.* I think they need to know from my firsthand experience that heaven is real. Because I can say, "I made a roundtrip this time. Next time, I'll have a one-way ticket," they understand. They long for the assurance of that future reality.

They hear about heaven in sermons and read about it in the Bible, but during those bleak and empty moments, they wonder. Something about my having been there seems exactly what they yearn to hear.

Third, they sense that because I understand pain, I can connect with their hurts. How could I not connect with them? But there are people in constant pain who don't understand it—they only endure it. As a follower of Jesus Christ I believe that God uses my pain to bring healing to others.

Because I stand before people—even with one leg shorter than the other—and talk to them about the reality of heaven, many of them focus on my suffering and translate it to their own situations.

Isn't that what we do with our faith? Isn't that how we interpret the Bible and especially eternal life? When we hear about the death of Jesus Christ, on some level, we grasp the point: The Perfect One who knew no sin became sin for us. He was beaten and crucified.

Sad to say, the story of Jesus is too often removed from the emotional grasp of many. They want to believe—and perhaps they do—but I know that once they read my books or hear my CDs or hear me speak, and then talk to me, they feel more assured.

So when I stand before them and say, "I've been there. I know the place the Perfect One has prepared for us," they're ready to listen.

As I wrote that, I realized that God sometimes refuses to give us what we want in order to give us what we need. I wanted total healing. I wanted to go back to my former way of life, but God chose differently. But now, because of my pain, I can understand the pain of others.

Throughout history, Paul's harsh experiences have been a blessing to the church. Otherwise the critics could have said, "How could Christianity have missed? It was upheld and spread by a man of commanding powers, without physical weaknesses, and no inner handicaps."

Instead the most effective witness for the gospel in those early years was a man who had been criticized, beaten, and despised. We assume he was a man with physical problems, but he was also a man of great power.

I'm not Paul, but I believe God uses my efforts and my life in a smaller but similar way.

At the same time, I wish my body didn't cry out all the time, I really do. But if this is what it takes for God to use me to heal others' hurts, I think I'm close to the attitude of Paul. After he begged for healing and God said his grace was enough, the apostle writes: "So now I am glad to boast about my weaknesses, so that the power of Christ can work through me. That's why I take pleasure in my weaknesses and in the insults, hardships, persecutions, and troubles that I suffer for Christ. For when I am weak, then I am strong" (2 Corinthians 12: 9b–10**).

I couldn't and wouldn't use all those descriptions of his weaknesses, but like the people who identify with me, I identify with Paul.

SEVENTEEN

We Might As Well Laugh

In the mid-1990s, many of us watched TV scenes of raging fires in Arizona. A reporter interviewed one of the state's top political figures (I think it was the governor). In the background we saw the blaze and heard about the thousands of acres already consumed.

"What happened to your state is terrible," the reporter said and gave viewers alarming statistics. He turned back to the politician. "How do you personally feel about this?"

Without hesitation, he said, "It's like getting hit by a big Mack truck."

In the summer of 2005, we seemed to have more hurricanes that struck the United States than I'd ever heard of in one year. Katrina and Rita are the two best known ones.

I flipped on the news one morning and heard a TV anchor from New York interview the mayor of a small town in Florida— I didn't get the name of the place, but the man spoke about the destruction and loss of property. He stood in front of a huge pile of rubble. He raised his fist and shook it. "We're going to rebuild and we're going to come back strong like all those people. We won't be defeated."

"What's that behind you?" the news anchor asked. "What's that big pile of rubble behind you?"

The mayor looked down momentarily and said in a quivering voice, "That's what's left of my house."

"That's your house? You mean you lost your house?"

He didn't answer, but nodded.

"For just a minute, forget that you're the mayor. As a person, how does this make you feel?"

The mayor stroked his chin a couple of times before he said, "Well, really, it's like getting hit by a big truck."

I sat in the living room with my wife, Eva, and Chris, one of my sons.

"Dad, did you hear that?"

"Yeah, I heard it."

"Can you believe that man said that?"

"Yes and no. I guess I can believe he searched for something that people would identify with. But no I can't believe my experience is the standard for misery."

Then I laughed because I saw the humor in the situation. In fact, if we can't see the humor it shows we haven't coped with the situation. I don't know how people manage to struggle through their ordeals if they can't see the humor in their lives.

Here's another example. Eva has taught in the public schools since 1974. Because of tragedies around the country, the schools have strengthened security. I don't always get to meet the entire faculty at her school, even though she's taught at that particular one for several years.

One day I went to visit her shortly after school had been dismissed. Most of the teachers knew me, so they waved or greeted me. I walked down the hallway toward her classroom. Because they knew me, no one challenged me as they're trained to do. However I saw a teacher I didn't know and nodded to her and kept on walking.

"Excuse me, sir," she said. "May I help you?"

"Yes, I'm Don Piper and I'm here to see my wife, Eva."

"Oh, Eva, okay. She's in her classroom and that's—"

"I know where it is."

She smiled at me and I walked on. I went to Eva's classroom but she wasn't there and I wondered where she could be. Her car was still in the parking lot. I decided that she had probably gone to the teachers' lounge, so I headed in that direction. I turned a corner and saw Eva coming my way.

"Oh, there you are," Eva said.

"Wait a minute, that was my line," I answered. "I've been looking for you."

"Susie [the other teacher], told me you were here."

"I didn't know her—"

"She didn't know you, either," Eva said. "But she told me, 'Your husband is here.' And I asked, 'Are you sure it's my husband?' And she said, 'Yes, he's tall and limping.' And I said, 'Oh, that's him.'"

Both of us laughed. "That sounds like an Indian name, doesn't it? There's Dances with Wolves, but I'm Tall Limping Man."

After that, several members of the faculty began to call me Tall Limping Man. And I laugh because it's funny. It's sad that I'm limping, but I decided long ago that I had to lighten up.

So I'm trying to see things that are funny. I've learned that when we can laugh, it helps the whole process of finding the new normal become a little bit easier. We'll cross over that bridge with a little bit lighter load. It won't be quite as painful and devastating and awful. You know what? I've learned that when we laugh at ourselves, we also help the people around us because they're worried about us. They want to do something to make life better for us. When they see us emotionally down it scares them. But if we can laugh at our situation occasionally, it helps them laugh and their load is also lighter.

Cecil Murphey, my cowriter, has a good friend named Chris Maxwell. In 1996, Chris contracted viral encephalitis (the medical term for inflammation of the brain). The medical experts never discovered the cause, but the major result is that Chris irretrievably lost his short-term memory.[5] Today he carries a PalmPilot around and makes constant notes.

When the two of them meet, Cec often says, "I'm surprised you remember me." Chris laughs but admits there was a time when he would have cried over those words. But he's now able to grasp the humor. That shows he has been healed.

Here's another example. My brother-in-law, Eddie Pentecost, is a singer and guitarist. Several of us in the family sat around one day while he played and sang. The lyrics of one of the songs mentioned getting hit by a big truck. He sang away and we listened to him. As soon as he finished the section about the truck, he stopped and blurted out, "Oh, I didn't even think about that."

I laughed and joined in the song with him. As we continued, I made up lines about the truck and the family had a laugh marathon.

---

[5] He records his story in his memoir, *Changing My Mind* (Franklin Springs, GA: LifeSprings Resources, 2005).

Some people might have thought we'd lost our minds. I thought it was funny and I could enjoy the humor of the moment. I was spontaneously letting them know I'm okay. I don't want people to watch their words around me or feel I'll be offended if they make jokes about big trucks.

Yes, my accident was a horrible experience, but I think of the old line that goes, "If you don't laugh, you'll probably cry." I've put it in perspective. The truck didn't kill me—I mean, it did, but I'm alive now. The experience didn't debilitate me to the point where I can't function anymore. I celebrate success in overcoming the physical hardships.

I say to people in pain and with disabilities, "If you can laugh at something, you can defeat it. If you can laugh, it doesn't conquer you but you have conquered it."

One of my favorite TV moments was when I watched a program where Ray Charles and Stevie Wonder walked on the stage. Both men are blind, of course, and one came from stage left and the other from stage right. They bumped into each other and then did a nice, humorous exchange. As they finished, Ray Charles said, "Hey, Stevie, nice to see you again."

"Yeah, nice seeing you, too." They shook hands and walked off in the opposite direction.

I roared. The scene probably wasn't that funny to most people. It was hilarious to me. Both men were able to make a big joke out of their blindness.

I've had a few critical comments about my laughing, but I decided that if I couldn't laugh at myself, I'd live in a continuously devastated life.

Heaven is a serious topic to me. It's the most important place in the world and no one gets there by accident. It's not a subject we might ordinarily joke about, but I want to share one story.

One time I was in a large church just outside Baton Rouge and I spoke about heaven and eternal life. I said it was the most glorious, exciting, happy thing we could possibly contemplate. "Everything in heaven is perfect. Every person in heaven is perfect. When you get there, you'll be exactly the way God wanted you to be when he created you in the first place. We're ageless and perfect."

Just then a man stood up and yelled something. I couldn't hear what he said so I asked him to repeat it.

"I want to know about hair."

He certainly caught me off guard. I wasn't used to that kind of interruption and I just said, "Excuse me, sir?"

"I want to know about hair."

"I'm sorry, I don't understand."

"Did the people in heaven have hair?" He was follicle deprived—bald.

I had to stop and think a little bit; that's not something I had ever thought about. I said, "Yes, as best as I can remember everybody in heaven had hair."

He looked upward, raised his arms, and yelled "Praise God!" He sat down.

That wasn't the response I wanted, but it was a fun break. It took me several minutes to get control again.

Here's another story. In the summer of 2006, a woman approached me after the worship service. "I was just struck by what you shared about heaven and how glorious it is," she said. "I do have a question."

"What's your question?"

"I would like to know if in heaven it would be possible that I could be a size two?" And she wasn't anywhere close to a size two.

Several people stood behind her and were smiling at her question. As humorous as it sounded, I took it seriously. "I don't know," I said. "I can tell you this much: You will be the way God wants you to be and it'll be wonderful. It will be wonderful because it will be perfect. But I can't promise you a size two."

She thought for a minute, obviously disappointed, and then she smiled, "If I'll be perfect that's good enough for me."

It's interesting what people's goals in heaven are, if they want hair, if they want to be smaller, or whatever they want to be. On earth we seem to be enamored with such things. We spend billions on cosmetics and health care and this reduction and that plastic surgery, and those will be simply nonexistent in heaven. We'll be perfect and we'll love being exactly the way we are. God loves us the way we are and he made us that way. So it's interesting to think about our priorities.

Another time, somebody waited in line for two hours to ask me a question. I did a book signing at a Books-A-Million store. Near the end of the line a woman who had apparently been there the whole time finally made her way up to the table where I was. I looked up at her and apologized for her having to wait so long. "We didn't anticipate this many people."

"Oh, that's okay. But I do have a question for you."

"Well, okay, what's your question?"

"There's something I've always wondered."

"Okay."

She leaned across the desk and with great gravity said, "I would like to know if while you were in heaven you saw Elvis?"

My first reaction was to look around to see if there were any cameras. Maybe this was a joke and we were on television. Then I realized that she was absolutely serious. "You know, I didn't see Elvis, although I've always been a big Elvis fan. But remember, the people I met at the gates of heaven were those I knew. They were people who had helped me get to heaven. While Elvis was certainly a great singer and a wonderful person, I didn't see him there. Now that doesn't mean he's not maybe inside waiting for us there."

"Oh, I hope so."

"I do, too. I really do honestly hope so," I said. "Truly, I hope everyone goes to heaven. I'm about the business of trying to invite everybody into heaven."

We shook hands, I signed her book, and she smiled before she left.

Months later I spoke at the First Baptist Church in Bossier City, just across the Red River from Shreveport. Elvis spent a great deal of the first part of his career singing at a place called the Louisiana Hayride in Shreveport. I spoke at First Baptist Church, the church where I had grown up, so it was a historic day for me. I returned to speak in the pulpit at the church where I became a Christian and had been baptized.

Thousands attended that day and we had a marvelous service. I went out to the lobby to do another book signing. I spotted the pastor of the church and he stood in line. I wondered why because I'd given him a book earlier. There was certainly no reason for him to stand in line. I was taken aback and said, "Pastor, you're in line."

"Yes, I want you to meet somebody." And he moved out of the way and standing there was an older couple. And he said, "I would like to introduce you to somebody."

"You don't have to introduce me, I know who he is." He was James Burton.

I stood up to shake hands with him and the man said, "I enjoyed your book. It really meant a lot to me."

"Well, thank you, and that's very kind, I appreciate that," I said. "I want to shake the hand of the man who played the lead guitar for Elvis Presley and I'm really glad to meet you."

"No, I'm glad to meet you."

James Burton is a legend in the music industry and had stopped by to tell me how much he liked my book.

"I've got to tell you something," I said. He leaned close and I told him the story about the woman who waited two hours. "She asked me if I saw Elvis in heaven." And I said, "I had to tell her I didn't because the people I saw were people who helped me get there."

And he threw his head back and laughed before he said. "But you know, Elvis is there."

"He is?"

"Oh yes, I was with him when he became a Christian. There's no question in my mind he was an authentic believer. In spite of the troubles he had in the later part of his life and the drugs and all of that, he knew who he was and he knew where he was going. So Elvis was a Christian, and he is in heaven."

And I thought, I wish that woman would have asked the question about Elvis tonight.

EIGHTEEN

Helping and Being Helped

I learned an invaluable lesson through my accident and I learned
it in two different ways.

Before my accident, I was a competent, independent person. I
was a minister—and I took that job seriously. I helped people. That's
what I did as a profession and that's what I did because I genuinely
liked people and I believed God had called me to do that.

And I did minister. I put in more hours than my job required.
That's not unusual because I think that's true with most pastors
and ministers of every kind. We don't keep our eyes on the clock,
but we keep our hands reaching out to help.

That strength—that desire to help—was also my weakness. I
liked being a helper; I didn't like being helped. If anyone in need
called or asked for me, I was there. Again I think that's typical of
most of us in the helping profession.

My first lesson came as a serious rebuke from an older, retired minister named Jay B. Perkins. He visited me often in the
hospital and when he saw how independent I tried to be while

I was still a patient, he let me have it verbally. He sat at my side when friends or members of the South Park church visited. Almost all of them asked if they could do something for me and I would tell them no.

One day Jay waited until a visitor left, walked to my bed, stared at me, and said loudly, "You need to get your act together."

I had no idea what he meant.

He bent down close to me and said, "You're a raging hypocrite."

I didn't have any idea what stirred him up.

"Those people care about you. You can't imagine how deeply they love you."

I tried to protest and said I knew that.

"Really? Well, you're not doing a good job of letting them know you're aware." He gave me quite a lecture and his point was that they wanted to help—just to do something for me, anything— and I wouldn't let them.

When I protested that I didn't want them to do anything, that's when he really let me have it. "It's not your call." He went on to point out that I'd spent my life trying to help others. Here's the one statement he said that burned inside me: "It's the only thing they have to offer you, and you're taking that gift away from them."

I wish I could say I screamed in delight, "Yes, yes! I get it." Instead I said I understood, but I didn't—not really. It took a couple of weeks for me to truly grasp what Jay B. Perkins meant. I finally learned: I *allowed* others to help.

It's still not easy for me, but I am getting better. I realize that if I withhold from them, I cheat them out of the opportunity to minister to me. I deprive them of the ability to prove their love by their actions.

There's a second way I grasped this truth of being open to others wanting to help. I've described my trip to heaven in previous books. The people who met me at the gate were people who had influenced my life and had died. Because of them, I had lived as a Christian from the age of sixteen until the age of thirty-eight when the accident took place.

As I reflected on meeting with them, especially after the searing words from Jay B. Perkins, I thought: I allowed those people to influence me. That means they helped me. They were all joy filled at the gate because they had impacted my life in some way.

Will there be people at the gate who ought to greet me after I cross the final bridge? Will the people be there who wanted the opportunity—just a small chance—to show their love and God's love?

As I have slowly learned to accept my responsibility to receive help, I'm in a stronger position to say it both ways to people. Be helpers of those in need, be recipients of their help when you're in need.

If we look at the life of the apostle Paul (and others) that's exactly how it worked. Paul tirelessly gave himself to others. He did everything he could for them.

But he also received. To the Philippians he wrote, "As you know, you Philippians were the only ones who gave me financial help when I first brought you the Good News and then traveled on from Macedonia. No other church did this. Even when I was in Thessalonica you sent help more than once. I don't say this because I want a gift from you. Rather, I want you to receive a reward for your kindness" (Philippians 4:15–17**).

I want to show how this works in our daily lives. We don't have to do big things. Offering help means that we care and out of that care we act. It's really that simple.

For example, in my previous writings, I've mentioned Papa—my grandfather—who died many years ago. He was the first person I saw when I reached heaven.

Papa and my grandmother had been married forty-nine years before his death. After he was gone, she went into such a tailspin that we couldn't get her to leave the house.

For months, the only time she left the house was once a day to go to the cemetery and visit Papa's grave. It was as if her life stopped and she had only one daily task—to visit his grave. Beyond that, my grandmother had nothing else of interest to her. We tried to gently discuss that with her and she would listen to us, and then say, "I need to visit Joe [Papa] every day."

"That's fine, but you need to do other things." In her own way she had closed off her life to the rest of the world.

All of us family members were concerned so we talked to some of her friends. My grandmother had driven a school bus for thirty-one years and actually had a few instances of driving three generations of kids. She was greatly loved in the community. We talked to other retired school bus drivers. They were aware of not seeing her around but they hadn't thought much about the reason. They were shocked to realize how she had isolated herself. They decided to help my grandmother.

They started by inviting her to lunch. She refused, of course, so two or three would come to the house and beg. "Bonnie, we love you," they said. "You're a wonderful person to be with. You're depriving us of your fellowship. We want to be with you. We enjoy being with you, and Joe wouldn't want you to sit around the house and he sure wouldn't want you to come out to the cemetery every day. He'd worry about that. He wants you to have a life."

She still refused. So two or three got together, visited my grandmother, and refused to leave. "Come and go with us to lunch." They paid no attention to her protests. "We'll stay here all day if we have to." They finally forced her to get dressed and go with them. They didn't give her any choice.

That was such a crucial step in her recovery. They not only offered but they insisted even when she refused. They did that because they cared. Their love for her was stronger than her refusal to leave the house.

They got her into the habit of going out to lunch with them, so they decided to go on to the next step. The retired school bus drivers decided to charter buses for long trips. That was amazing: They hired someone to drive them from Louisiana to Canada, California, or New England. They insisted that my grandmother go with them. When she argued, they didn't listen, and they wouldn't take her refusal as a final answer.

They pointed out that none of them had to drive and they could finally be tourists on a bus. They constantly talked to her of the fun they would have. Reluctantly she went the first time. She came back a changed woman and from that moment on, she was my grandmother again.

It's not that she didn't go to Papa's grave anymore, but the trip became a weekly occurrence and eventually even a monthly visit. She didn't remember or love Papa any less. Those women helped my grandmother get on with the rest of her life and she had a good life after that. They gave themselves to her and forced her to accept their help.

The New Testament often speaks of the church as a body, such as in 1 Corinthians 12:12–26. Paul uses that image to show how much we need to learn to depend on each other and to reach out to those who need us. He wanted the church then—and the church today—to realize that we weren't created to be independent of each other.

I recently heard a story about a woman in an assisted living home. She was bitter because she wanted to stay in her own house, even though she wasn't physically able to take care of herself. At her new residence, she kept to herself and refused to have anything to do with anyone.

When no one was around, she would sneak down to the recreation room, close all the doors, and play the piano, often at two in the morning. She assumed no one knew she could play the piano.

One man who lived down the hall from her came up to her and said, "I need your help."

She started to refuse, but he wasn't going to let her refuse. "I love to sing, but I get off-key," he said. "I need music. I've heard you play. Sometimes I can't sleep so I get up and walk. The other night I stood outside the door and listened. You have a beautiful touch."

"I don't play for anyone but myself," she said.

"Please, will you play a song for me? Just one? I'm a baritone and I had some voice training but it's been so long since I've sung that I can't do it without accompaniment. I agreed to sing at our next worship service. And you know we don't have anyone who can play."

The woman gave him many excuses but he kept saying, "I know it's an imposition, but please, just one song."

She finally gave in and played for him. Most people can figure out the rest of the story because it worked. In asking for her help, he helped her get out of withdrawal. It took months but she finally adjusted to the facilities there.

Oh, there's one minor thing. She began to play again regularly and at age eighty-three, she married the baritone. They shared almost a year of life together before he died, but it was enough to awaken her. For the next year or two before she died, she was the one who greeted every newcomer and made them feel welcome.

Because she had been tricked into receiving help, she became a helper. Sometimes that's how it has to work.

I've realized that helping can sometimes be a simple thing. How about inviting a single parent and the children over for a meal during the holidays? Take a shut-in shopping or offer to do some shopping for them. One of the complaints I hear from women is that after their husbands die, their friends evaporate. They feel as if other women think they'll try to steal their husbands. Why not reach out to someone like that? If we want to help, we'll find ways.

And to those who, like me, didn't want people to help them, my advice comes in two words: *Let them.* Let them help you because they want to or they wouldn't have asked. Just smile and thank them and let them.

A final word here: Pride may be the problem of refusing help. Most people—including Don Piper—like to think of themselves as able to take care of their own needs and not to depend on someone else. To receive help humbles us and some of us don't like that. A lot of my pride got smashed after my accident and it still took years before I honestly learned to appreciate what others wanted to do for me.

Again, to the Philippians Paul pleaded with the people to "make my joy complete by being like-minded . . ." (Philippians 2:2[†]) and then went on to say, "Each of you should look not only to your own interests, but also to the interests of others" (Verse 4). If I refuse to let someone help me, I'm disobeying the command of God right here: I refuse to allow them to look out for me or to help me.

I've come to the conclusion that humility is a quality God loves. The more we're aware of our needs, the more we depend on God and God uses people to minister to our needs. Life is about giving and sharing of ourselves.

NINETEEN

The Bridge of Compassion

Before my trip to heaven, I would have resented it if anyone had said I wasn't compassionate. I did care about people. I would never have become a pastor if I hadn't cared.

But heaven changed me. I came out of that experience a different person. It was as if I had gone across a bridge from being a kind, caring person and come out on the other side with a heart of compassion. I don't mean to imply that I bleed with pain for every person I meet. I do mean I care on a deeper level than I ever thought possible.

I can't explain the reason for the change and I'm not sure I can explain the change. Perhaps it was because I stood among a perfected group of people in heaven and the radiance of those moments changed me. As I've reviewed that experience, the memory takes away the pettiness, the judgmental attitude toward others. Those things that used to irritate me and upset me evaporated from my memory.

I'm still human and sometimes I lapse back into my old ways, but I know—I truly know—the difference between feeling concern and feeling compassion. I don't think we have to go to heaven to have that kind of change. Whenever any of us has a life-shattering experience, one positive result that can come out of it is compassion. It's not that we were cruel, hard-hearted, or unfeeling before, but the experience changes us. Perhaps part of it is that we have experienced events that give us a different outlook on life.

For example, one time a woman came to me and said, "I simply couldn't understand about people going through divorce. If they're both Christians, how can they possibly break up? All they have to do is pray and ask God to help."

I listened to her, trying to frame an answer. I didn't need to say anything.

"Six months ago, after twenty-one years of marriage, my husband demanded a divorce. He said he had prayed and talked to our pastor, but he grew even more miserable." She broke into tears before she trusted her voice enough to speak again. "Now I understand about divorce. I've been there."

How is it possible to feel the pain and suffering of another person? We can't feel it physically as they do, but we can remember our pain and our suffering. Like the woman who went through a divorce—she understands. She can feel the pain others go through.

Some people may be naturally compassionate. For me, it was a learned experience. I lay in the hospital for nearly four months after my accident. During those days, I learned a great deal about myself—and much of it I didn't want to know. I was able to recognize the worst side of myself. At times I was ashamed of my behavior, my pettiness, and my insensitivity. But I also realized something positive: Even at my worst, my family still loved me;

my friends stayed with me; the church didn't desert me. Most of all, God hadn't rejected me.

In reflection (and reflection can only come after the event) I now look back at my own difficulties and remember. Because I remember, I can translate those painful days into understanding the pain and difficulties others go through.

Members of groups such as Alcoholics Anonymous sometimes say to people like me, "You don't know how it is to be addicted to alcohol." Perhaps they're right and I don't argue, but maybe I understand more than they think. I don't understand addiction, but I do understand pain. I understand what it's like to hurt—physically and emotionally. I understand what it's like to want to take something so the hurt won't feel so bad.

Recovering addicts of all kinds are often so taken up with their own problems of recovery, of crawling out of the hole, of moving beyond yearning for another fix, they can see little else. At that stage, they're correct: I can't understand. I also want to say that it probably takes all their energies and resolve to make those first steps. They're not ready to care about anyone else. They need to focus on their own pain.

But once they move beyond the first stage, once they live on a level beyond mere sobriety, they begin to realize they are not quite so unique after all. It doesn't matter whether the subject is addiction, temptation, pain, or blessing, none of us is truly unique. We may feel we are, but if we're open to ourselves, we soon learn differently. In the early days—the days of recovery or seeking the new normal, we usually feel as if no one else has ever walked down the same path. We can't hear other people because we're too focused on ourselves and our trauma or even on our blessings.

We *need* to have a time when we feel unique, different, and separate from the rest of the world. During that transition time, we feel the most negative thoughts and assume no one else in the entire universe has ever felt quite the same way. It's not a logical response; it's an emotional response. And in truth, we really don't care if others have felt the same way. It's as if to say, "This is my unique time when I feel totally different from anyone else. No one can possibly understand."

If we're willing to move forward, we recognize that we did go through a transition stage. Once we got whatever we needed from licking our wounds, feeling sorry for ourselves, isolating ourselves from others, we're ready to move back into the real world again.

But we don't reenter the way we went out. Something has changed within us. At first we may not be aware of the adjustment and sometimes those transformations may be subtle, but we are different.

Two things strike me about moving out of the period of isolation. *First, we're softer. We're kinder, less demanding, not as judgmental.* We all come out differently, but we do come out different.

A twenty-four-year-old man, whom I'll call Chip, wrote me a poignant e-mail:

"I must say that I thoroughly enjoyed your book, *90 Minutes in Heaven*. It was a great source of comfort to me and my walk with God. I have been a Christian and have had God in my heart since I was fourteen—which was ten years ago. I'm at a point in my life where I want more of God in my life. I want to know God more and to feel his presence because I know it's possible. I've had my own set of struggles that in no way relate to your physical struggles, but they have tested me to the core. I found myself losing my relationship with God and I didn't care. It wasn't until I was at my lowest point that the only thing I could do was look back up. And that's what I have done.

"I was in my own kind of emotionally and spiritually damaging 'car wreck' a year ago. I lost the love of my life, my girlfriend, who I met in college. She was the first girl I ever kissed. Much of our two-and-a-half-year relationship was spent together. We prayed and talked about God in our lives. I later learned that throughout the course of our relationship she cheated on me. She would say she loved me and then cheat on me when I wasn't around. When I found out, the ordeal left me broken in so many aspects that I felt I needed my own 'Ilizarov' to put me back together.

"I tell you this because I'm thankful for your book helping me to understand God's ability to comfort. I love the fact you put 2 Corinthians 1:3–4[6] in your book as well.

"This year I have grown up and matured at a rate I never thought was possible and I hope to continue on this path. We don't always understand why things happen, but I know that I can comfort anyone who has ever been cheated on in a relationship. I strongly believe that to be my purpose for having experienced such a devastating relationship."

That young man understood something in retrospect—through painful experience—and that's the way we have to learn so many of life's lessons. As we understand suffering in ourselves, we can grasp suffering in others.

The second aspect of coming out of isolation is that we come

---

[6] "Praise be to the God and Father of our Lord Jesus Christ, the Father of compassion and the God of all comfort, who comforts us in all our troubles, so that we can comfort those in any trouble with the comfort we ourselves have received from God." [†]

out of the experiences wiser. We didn't know all the answers to all the problems before our painful, shattering events, but we acted and felt as if we knew most of them. As we reemerge, we feel less confident that we know everything.

We're wiser in just that regard. If we've learned, we've become slower to criticize, quicker to listen, and more open to accept.

As I reflect regularly on my accident and the lessons I've learned, I'm grateful. I wish I could have learned them without pain and hardship. But I did learn. That's what's important.

If we truly have learned, we never forget the events that changed our lives. If it was painful or joyful, we lose the sharpness of the images in our minds. Our minds have a marvelous way to dismiss the negative and emphasize the positive.

For example, my cowriter had a bad experience with another missionary just before he left Africa. The untrue accusations from a man he had respected hurt him deeply. As the years passed, the pain lessened. Ten years later, he said, "I can't remember the words. Even the untrue accusations seem less important today."

That is, he had moved beyond the trauma. They were of the past and they stayed in the past. The influence of those memories, however, affected him strongly. He struggled to forgive the other missionary and in the process realized he, too, had made mistakes. Part of his role was to forgive himself.

That's where compassion truly begins: We need to forgive ourselves for our failures. As I said above, when I realized my shortcomings, I was ashamed. I truly was. I never asked them, but I'm sure the people who loved me knew my failures and shortcomings. I know none of the revelations surprised God.

As I reflected, I also pondered the timing of the revelations that eventually produced more compassion. I can only say that God taught me at the time I was ready. In my case, I was confined to a bed and unable to stop thinking and examining my life.

Many times I've thought of a significant statement by Mordecai in the book of Esther. The girl, whom Mordecai had adopted, was brought to the Persian palace and later chosen as queen. At Mordecai's insistence, Esther kept her ethnic identity—her Jewishness—a secret. The Jews' enemy, Haman, convinced the king to allow the people to kill every Jew.

Mordecai set up a plan—one that involved some danger to Esther—to save the Jews from extinction in Persia. He said to her, "And who knows but that you have come to royal position for such a time as this?" (Esther 4:14b†). His plan worked, of course, but the point I want to make is the statement he made to Esther: "And who knows but that you have come to royal position for such a time as this?"

Who knows but that we have come to our place in life *for such a time as this?*

Your current situation may be God's secret weapon to accomplish great things. He works behind the scenes to enable us to fulfill His purpose.

Isn't that how God works? We learn compassion when we're ready. We learn to care when we're open to God's instructions. Our task is to learn the lessons at the right time.

If we're teachable, we become divine instruments in the world. That may sound like a grandiose statement, but I believe it. It's not whether we help two people or two million. What is important is that we change and then use the change in our lives to reach out.

I can think of nothing more God's people need today than compassion. For me, compassion means an awareness of another's pain accompanied with a desire to do something to alleviate it.

I'm sometimes introduced to audiences as the Minister of Hope, and I confess I like that. Part of that idea of hope, however, is that I've learned to care about the plight and the pain of others. I want to do what I can to help alleviate those hurts. That's why compassion is important to me.

TWENTY

Choosing to Give Thanks

For 105 days, I lay in a hospital bed. My life as I had known it was shattered. Although I felt grateful to be alive, I also struggled with depression, which is not that unusual with such trauma. My body was a physical mess and I would never again be the healthy thirty-eight-year-old man I once had been.

Somewhere during those weeks in the hospital and during the months of recuperation at home, I slowly accepted reality. Life wouldn't wait for me. I had to do something to make my life have meaning once again. I had no way to know how much physical mobility I would have, but I couldn't just focus on my pain and problems.

During that time, I read my Bible, and the fourth chapter of the book of Philippians began to take on new meaning. I have no idea how many times I had read the passage before, but I finally read it as words that spoke to me, a message from God to speed me on my way toward the new normalcy.

Paul wrote from prison to Christians who may have been

undergoing persecution. That was one thing that amazed me. Instead of feeling sorry for himself, he exhorted others to move forward. The Romans had imprisoned him, and Paul could have complained. Instead, in Chapter 2 he starts with these words: "If you have any encouragement from being united with Christ . . ." (Verse 1†). He mentions the love, fellowship, tenderness, and compassion that spring from our relationship to the Lord, before he added that if they had any of those qualities, "Then make my joy complete by being like-minded, having the same love, being one in spirit and purpose" (Verse 2). He exhorted them to be united and to care for one another.

The more I read those words, the more amazing they seemed. This man had every reason to feel sorry for himself. He was in prison and faced death, but physical death wasn't the issue on his mind. Instead he wanted to encourage the believers in Philippi.

Then I read the list of physical suffering Paul went through as he records in 2 Corinthians 11:18–29. Yes, Paul knew physical suffering. He also knew the pain of rejection, of not being believed, of heaviness over the failings of others. "Besides everything else, I face daily the pressure of my concern for all the churches. Who is weak, and I do not feel weak? Who is led into sin, and I do not inwardly burn?" (Verses 28–29†). Paul had certainly suffered many hardships.

As I read and reread the four chapters of Philippians, I gained some perspective on Paul's life and his tremendous compassion for others.

In the final chapter, Paul gives a series of exhortations to the Philippian Christians. The part that touched me most deeply begins with these words: "Rejoice in the Lord always. I will say it again: Rejoice! Let your gentleness be evident to all. The Lord is near. Do not be anxious about anything, but in everything by prayer and petition, with thanksgiving, present your requests to God" (4:4–6).

To start with giving thanks in the midst of persecution and uncertainty sounds odd and perhaps presumptuous. How can we be thankful when our world has collapsed or turned upside down? How can we give thanks when gripped by problems, hardships, and pain?

Paul says, in effect, "I've considered everything that can possibly happen. I've pondered death and I've contemplated life. Christian joy is independent of everything on earth. It's that way because God's Holy Spirit is with us."

We have promises all through the Bible that God never leaves us. If the Holy Spirit is an active part of our lives, we have spiritual resources to face whatever life throws at us.

The great apostle had experienced it all and he could still write to the Philippians and tell them to rejoice and to give thanks.

"If he knew how bad my life was," one woman told me, "he wouldn't say that."

"Yes, I think he would," I said. "In fact, his life was probably worse."

Paul's answer is simple: Just do it.

One thing I learned in finding my new normal was that I could discover ways in which to give thanks. Instead of focusing on my own pain and the terrible ordeal, I slowly moved out of that self-defeating cycle. I had to pause at times and remind myself of the things for which I could give thanks. Here are a few of them:

- I was alive.
- My family had stayed by me.

- My friends loved me.
- Members of our congregation did everything they knew to help us.
- People from all over the country contacted us and told us they prayed for me.
- The church kept me on as pastor.
- I learned to understand others better.

Some days it was difficult to give thanks. Some days I could barely focus on anything, but as I improved, my thoughts were freer. I found other things for which to be grateful—pain medication, nurses who treated me gently, friends who visited but didn't demand a lot of conversation, cards and letters that encouraged me.

I'm convinced we can *learn* to give thanks. And for many of us, it is a learning experience. We expect life to go a certain way and when it doesn't fit our expectations, it's easier to complain. However if we're going to accept our new life—our new normal—we have to make changes. Part of preparing ourselves for the new normal is to assess where we are and accept the present. Part of accepting the present is to admit that life isn't hopeless and that we don't have to live in despair.

One of the things that helped me in giving thanks and praise to God is the constant plea from the book of Psalms. For example, Psalm 103 is one of the best reasons given in the Bible for praising God:

- "May I never forget the good things he does for me" (Verse 2b†).
- "He forgives all my sins and heals all my diseases" (Verse 3).

- "He redeems me from death" (Verse 4a).
- "and crowns me with love and tender mercies" (Verse 4b).
- "He fills my life with good things" (Verse 5a).

The Bible is filled with such messages. Part of our growth is to learn to thank God and to live a life of joy.

Years ago, Cec Murphey, my cowriter, went through a particularly dark period in his life. "I learned to thank God for the simple things in life," he said. "We expect our lives to be happy, trouble free, and victorious. We forget that victories come only after we fight battles."

He made it a practice—and has continued it for at least a dozen years—that as soon as he awakens, he lies quietly and counts at least ten things for which he is truly thankful. At the time when life felt empty, he said it was difficult to find that many. Now he's gotten so much into the habit of thankfulness that it's normal and natural. "It has become almost automatic," he says, "to see the good and be thankful for everything in my life."

Cec's wife, Shirley, has serious physical problems. At church a concerned friend offered her sympathy for their situation. Cec thanked her and he added, without consciously thinking about it, "But you know, we've had so many good years together and we're thankful for them. Instead of looking at what we don't have anymore, I can rejoice in what God has done for us in the past."

That's the attitude Philippians 4 wants us to have. We begin with giving of thanks for life itself.

We take too many things for granted. One of the results of my trip to heaven is that I have a greater appreciation for what I once had, but also I understand that no matter how bad life is—or has been—it's absolutely nothing compared to the perfection that awaits us in heaven.

Elizabeth Kern e-mailed me and I felt she had such a spirit of giving of thanks despite the horrible story she had to tell.

"I wanted to let you know how much I enjoyed reading your book. After reading your story I felt a little better able to understand my husband's perspective. Early one morning, my oldest daughter's boyfriend decided to retaliate against her decision to break off their relationship. That man entered our home while we slept and shot my husband in the eye. Through the quick response of a neighbor, and the Life Flight to another hospital, my husband received excellent medical care from a talented brain surgeon.

"You said that you believed you survived due to 'relentless, passionate, and desperate' prayers. Many of Ron's friends and family felt the same way. (I am sorry to say that in my shock and fear I did not hold the same vision and prayed for God's will.) Our experience also brought us to our knees and maybe that is where God wanted us to be!

"We, too, were blessed by church family—actually two: Ron was a member of Holy Ghost Lutheran Church and I was at St. Joseph Catholic. For several months the two church families coordinated bringing us meals. The whole community even sponsored an auction for us.

"About six months after Ron was shot, he was determined to go back to church. On Easter Sunday, with a bucket in his lap in case he should become ill, Ron sat through the service.

"The brain injury he sustained affected so many aspects of his life. Yet, those of us close to him still saw a part of him as he was. He died five years after his injury and although I don't understand why God decided to take him home, I know he is in a better place.

"Ron hated being crippled. He couldn't drive, walk, read, and sometimes even eating was a struggle. He had changed both physically and mentally. We loved him anyway. I am sure your family and friends feel the same way."

That's the attitude of gratitude that all of us need. She could have moaned about what Ron had been, but instead she chose to focus on Ron as he was.

Isn't that always our choice? We can look at the things in life for which to be thankful or we can focus on our losses and our pains.

I'm on Paul's side. I choose to rejoice in the Lord *always*.

I have a friend who was sexually and physically abused in childhood. He went through an extreme amount of pain and much counseling, and thirty years later he said to me, "You know, I look back now and I can say that nobody ought to have to go through such experiences, but I honestly give thanks for my childhood because I like who I am now and I don't think I could have become me any other way."

That may be more than everyone can do, but it's a great example of what it means to give thanks and to hold on.

Am I thankful that I got hit by a big truck? On a spiritual level yes, because of all that it has taught me. And I'm grateful that my story of death-life-and-survival has benefited other people. Yes. I'm absolutely grateful for that.

Is it possible that I could have come to this place in my life in another way? Absolutely. Could I have had some other less painful experience that would have taught me these things? Probably not.

Perhaps it will help if I share a story I heard many years ago: A missionary in the South Pacific tried to teach the nationals to give freely to God. One Sunday, he missed one of his regular parishioners and no one knew where the man had gone. Days later, that absent man returned with a number of incredibly rare and beautiful seashells. It had taken him at least two days by foot to reach the ocean to find them. He presented the gifts to the missionary because he knew the church could sell them and bring in a lot of money. This was his contribution.

The missionary, deeply touched, said, "These are beautiful and you didn't have to go that far just to bring something to the church. You could have brought something from around here."

"No, the trip was part of the gift."

I think that tells my story well. Part of what I went through and I share with others is my gift. Do I recommend being hit by a truck? No, I don't recommend that but since it happened and it was very real and very vivid, yes, that's part of whatever gift I have to offer.

TWENTY-ONE

Learned Contentment

I don't want people to feel sorry for me; I had enough pity for myself at one point. But I do want to explain the hardship I faced after my accident and after I knew I would recover.

I would recover—that is, I would live, and I would learn to walk again—but I would never be free of pain. I would never be able to do dozens of easy things I had done all my life. I was thirty-eight years old when my physical world fell apart.

When my accident happened our twin sons were eight years old and our daughter, Nicole, was thirteen. I had always been a dad who interacted with his children. One of the hardest things for me to face was that I would never be able to play football with my twin sons. Maybe that's selfish, but it represented for me what I could *not* do.

When Nicole received an important award at South Park Baptist Church at thirteen years of age, I wasn't able to walk her down the aisle to receive it like the other dads did with their daughters. I didn't say much, but it broke my heart. The church was just happy I was able to be there that night. Rolling my wheelchair down the aisle with Nicole didn't have quite the same excitement.

I came from a military family and my dad had demonstrated unequivocally that men take care of their families and make decisions. But after my accident Eva had to make many of those decisions and handle the finances. As I expected, she made wise choices. That wasn't the problem. The problem was that I couldn't do my part.

I recount all of this because I see similar situations all the time as I travel from place to place. It was difficult for me to admit, "This is the way it is. It probably won't be better, because I probably won't get any better."

Much later, I read two statements that helped me. The first came from William James, the nineteenth-century man who pioneered psychology in the United States. He once wrote, "Acceptance of what has happened is the first step to overcoming the consequence of any misfortune."

A few years ago someone sent me an e-mail with a quote from the actress Mary Tyler Moore: "Pain nourishes courage. You can't be brave if you've only had wonderful things happen to you."

Those two statements have encouraged and challenged my thinking, but they didn't solve anything. The most help I received came from reading the book of Philippians, especially the fourth chapter. In the middle of that last chapter Paul thanks the people for their concern for his welfare during his imprisonment, even though they were unable to do anything to help. He wrote several amazing statements: "Not that I was ever in need, for I have learned how to be content with whatever I have. I know how to live on almost nothing or with everything. I have learned the secret of living in every situation, whether it is with a full stomach or empty, with plenty or little. For I can do everything through Christ, who gives me strength" (Philippians 4:11–13**).

As I thought of Paul's words, I tried to envision what his life was like. He was in prison and didn't know if he would survive or be killed, but that didn't upset him. Whether he had a lot of material things or none also seemed irrelevant.

I don't suppose I'll ever reach that point of which he spoke, but as I read his words again and again, the truth of what he wrote sank in.

My life wasn't going to get better. I would never have the strength, the energy, the health I had before I crossed that bridge. I could complain and make everyone else miserable or I could focus on what I could still do. I chose the latter.

That wasn't easy. But once I was able to admit that was how my life was and it probably wouldn't change a great deal, I accepted the situation. That's not quite contentment, but it shoved me along the right path. We need to accept our situation. But contentment involves more than just accepting; we need to be able to say, "If it never gets better, it's absolutely all right."

I didn't have a powerful experience where I yelled, "I'm content!" Mine was more gradual (maybe too gradual), but I finally *learned*. That's the truth: Over the years, I've learned to be content in all the circumstances where I find myself.

That statement sounds extraordinarily simple and it's essentially what the apostle Paul said. He said he had *learned* contentment and I think that's the only way anyone ever becomes contented.

Paul writes to the Philippians that his union with Jesus Christ infused him with the power or the ability to handle anything that came up in his life. The secret of his contentment was to depend on God. "For I can do everything through Christ, who gives me strength" (Verse 13).

Contentment isn't easily achieved—or at least it wasn't for me. I believe that by living in a world of fast change and all-pervasive advertisements, it's not easy to be content with what we have. Too many of us focus on what we don't have and worry about how we can get it. And once we get "it" (whatever it is we seek), a new discontent rises within us and we focus on one more thing that will make us happy.

As long as we put our energies on material things or achievements, we won't ever grasp what it means to be content. Contentment is an inside job. It's a work of grace. It means we have to depend on God. I learned to do that.

Frankly I didn't have a lot of choice. I couldn't be who I was before. I didn't want to make everyone around me miserable. As I slowly learned to accept what I could do and to accept my limitations, I was able to say, "Thank you, Lord, for what I can do."

In another chapter I write quite at length about the new normal—about accepting and adjusting to our new circumstances. We can aggressively pursue our new normal and be content at the same time. We can be content to know that we're moving ahead and that we're using the gifts God has given us.

It also means that we need to rejoice in our circumstances. That was hard, but I learned. Contentment relates to accepting it and rejoicing in it, practicing it, doing it, learning to really do it thoughtfully and joyfully and excitedly. I really had to work at this. I really fought against it. I questioned it. I went through a whole range of emotions but ultimately I've learned to be content; I accepted it.

When I finally hooked up with Cecil Murphey to write my first book, I did it in self-defense. I didn't want to talk about my situation or to go back over the past. I felt I had to get the book out and I just wanted to get it over with and be at peace.

After *90 Minutes in Heaven* came out and then *Daily Devotions Inspired by 90 Minutes in Heaven*, people responded. They told me of the impact I had made on their lives.

About once a week I receive an e-mail that goes something like this: "I hated my life." The person goes into detail and some of the circumstances are absolutely awful. The writer adds, "I was ready to take my own life." Sometimes the person talks about buying a gun or collecting enough pills to overdose. But in each case, the writer says in some way, "Because you shared your life, you have given me hope. I believe I can survive this tragedy."

Those responses help me in my struggle (and it's still a struggle) to be content. When I read such e-mails or hear people in my meetings, I'm amazed. I'm a middle-aged guy, I'm in bad physical shape, and sometimes I hurt so much it's hard to smile and talk. But I go out there and speak anyway. I do it because I believe that's what God has called me to do. And the payoff is the response I receive from others.

Then I'm content. I have done my best. I've done what I could do. Somehow the Holy Spirit has taken my simple words and impacted lives. I also realize that I could never have had such responses before my accident.

Because of where I have been and because I see so much pain in others, I don't want to run when someone says, "Don, I need to ask you about . . ."

I'm content to stop and listen. I'm able to answer whatever questions they have and I truly want to encourage them.

Beyond everything I've already said, I'm content because I know something I didn't understand before. I'm content because now I'm doing what I'm supposed to be doing with my life.

I get excited about the opportunities to share. How many people can hold the hand of wounded, desperate people and say, "Don't give up"? Those hurting people listen and they want words of guidance and encouragement. Sometimes I believe the Holy Spirit gives me wisdom to pass on to them. Every time it happens, I'm still shocked with joy—and I never want to get beyond that. I'm still deeply humbled by people who come to my meetings, who read my books, and who say, "Your life has made a difference in my life."

Heather Brodersen wrote: "My mother was in a horrible car accident and subsequently passed away two weeks later. She was a Christian and an avid reader. She mentioned your book to me about a month before her accident. I worked full-time and took night classes. I told her I didn't have time for a recreational read right then.

"Shortly after she died, I thought of her suggestion of reading your book. I am also a Christian (because of my mother's example) and have absolutely no doubt that my mom is with Christ in heaven. I bought your book because she wanted me to read it. As I read, it was as if she and you comforted me. I have an excitement for her and the glory she is experiencing for now and eternity!

"Because of your words of encouragement, I am at peace with my mother's passing. I never thought I would take it as well as I have. I believe you have helped with that."

Here's another example: I received an e-mail from a father

and he asked if he could call me. I was home for two days and I gave him permission to call me at home. Two years earlier his teenage son had accidentally shot himself and died. Once he recovered from his own grief, the father reached out to others and tried to offer them comfort. "I'm out of gas now," he said when he called.

I didn't think I had anything brilliant or inspirational to say to him. I spoke to him out of my contentment—out of relationship with Jesus, who empowers me. I wasn't aware of anything special that I did.

Just before he hung up, the man said, "These thirty minutes I've spent with you on the telephone have done me more good than months of trying to help other people." Again he told me that he had run out of gas. He was emotionally depleted and didn't know if he had done any good, which is why he contacted me.

"You encouraged me, Don, not only about heaven and knowing where my son is. You've helped me see that I can make a difference. I can wrap my arms around those other hurting parents who have gone through similar experiences."

Before we hung up, at least three more times, he said, "You really encouraged me."

I still don't know what I said that encouraged him, but that's not important. After I hung up, I felt a powerful sense of joy surge through me.

Could I ever have envisioned doing that before this accident? No. I would have said some nice words to the father. I would have prayed with him and I would have told him, "I will continue to pray for you. Call me if you need me." And I would have meant those words.

But this was a totally different conversation. It was a brother-to-brother, heart-to-heart, emotion-to-emotion thing where we connected in a way that is truly beyond any attempt at explanation.

That man hurt and felt forlorn. But he found a fellow struggler who had experienced enough pain on earth and joy in heaven that we could connect. We wept together and I could assure him that his son was totally happy in heaven.

I could also assure him of the truthfulness of Paul's words: "So, my dear brothers and sisters, be strong and immovable. Always work enthusiastically for the Lord, for you know that nothing you do for the Lord is ever useless" (1 Corinthians 15:58**).

I also found additional strength and joy in talking to him—and that resulted in an even greater level of contentment to me. God has used me to lift another's burden. Yes, I can do all things through the strength of Christ, and I can also be content because I know I'm *exactly* where God wants me to be.

TWENTY-TWO

Just Hold On

During my early days in the hospital they used to come to get me for physical therapy. The first time they decided to work on my standing, it took quite a few minutes, but I finally stood upright for the first time in weeks. Nausea threatened me and I felt incredibly sick because my equilibrium had totally rearranged itself. My body had to learn to readjust so I could handle the physical change and stand upright. To learn to walk again was a slow, painful process. Because my arm had been badly mangled, I needed to work to regain the use of my hand and arm as well. They gave me a red rubber ball to squeeze with my fingers. It hurt to do that, but if I wanted to get better, I knew I had to patiently participate. It took a great deal of effort to hold on to that ball and endure the pain. Over time the pain lessened, but it took a long time.

It required patience to squeeze that ball—something just about any child could do, but I didn't have the muscles of a child. I had to learn not only to hold on, but to endure.

That's one of the significant messages I have to offer: Hold on. Don't let go or give up. Just hold on.

When I lay in the ICU with pneumonia, the doctor came in and badgered me into breathing into the treatment tube. I didn't want to breathe; it hurt to try. But they cared and wanted me to live. They insisted that I had to get my lungs cleared. I wasn't patient then. I wanted to be over the agony and the awful efforts just to take a normal breath. I wanted to walk again; I wanted to be able to use my arm again. But I learned to hold on—not easily and not consistently—but I learned.

Patience is absolutely critical. If we don't develop and practice staying with the heavy things that weigh us down, we don't make progress. I've known people who had massive surgical procedures and afterward they wanted to skip over the physical therapy. They just wanted to feel good and jump past everything else.

To hold on means to grab something and not let go. I think of the exhortation in Hebrews 12:1: "Let us strip off every weight that slows us down. . . . And let us run with endurance the race that God has set before us."**

Whatever our particular weight, issue, or problem, we can't just cast them off and walk away. We often have to endure a lot of hardships and trial-and-error methods before we make it. When the nurse laid that rubber ball in my hands, it looked like such a simple thing to do. And now it is. But then, just to exert pressure from my fingers required immense concentration and energy. I had to learn there was only one way to get the muscles in my arms to work again. And I had to hold on and endure as I slowly built up my strength.

I remember a story about a farmer's son who just loved animals. He would help his father feed the pigs, milk the cows, and collect the eggs from the henhouse. One day he found a bird's nest with an egg in it. He called his father over, and soon they were delighted to see the egg crack and a little bird begin to struggle its way out. The little boy wanted to help the bird crack its shell, but his father stopped him. The boy just wanted to make things easier for the baby bird, but the farmer explained that to do the work for the bird impedes its growth. In fact, if he interfered, he might actually kill the chick. It gains strength by pecking its way out of the shell.

The story illustrates what is often so true: The struggle is necessary. It takes patience, and sometimes all we can do is just hold on. But we have to do the task at the right time, and we have to endure. God never promises that life will be easy. His exhortation to us is to just keep on and not give up.

But Paul writes in Colossians that with the Lord's power we can endure. "We also pray that you will be strengthened with all his glorious power so you will have all the endurance and patience you need. . . ." (1:11**). God can give us the strength to endure—and he does. In our struggle to hold on, we can turn to Jesus and he will be beside us. He understands our pain and our struggles because he was a man who suffered great agony. "Since he himself has gone through suffering and testing, he is able to help us when we are being tested" (Hebrews 2:18).

He's also able to help us when we want to give up. Our job is to hold on. Because the Lord is with us, we *can* endure.

One lesson I've learned from my ordeal is that I've encouraged others to hold on. I didn't do it for them, but in holding on for myself, my life has encouraged them.

Here's an e-mail from Eran Jones:

"A member of our church gave me a copy of *90 Minutes in*

Heaven. In September 2005, I underwent a spinal fusion of three discs in my lower back, complete with all the screws, rods, pins, and plates. The bone grafts from my hips were no picnic, either, as you well know. It has been a painful recovery and I still have a long way to go.

"First I was bedridden, then on a walker, and now I'm finally able to walk on my own. I thank God daily for letting me continue to do his work with his children.

"After reading your book, God opened my heart and spoke to me through your testimony. I know He has a plan for my life and I am trying hard to follow it. I am the Youth Ministry Assistant at First United Methodist Church. I know how difficult it must have been for you by my own experiences. Thank you for your words of inspiration to keep going. I, too, was depressed, but your book has rejuvenated me and I *will* press on. I am glad he gave you a glimpse of Heaven, but I am also glad he let you come back to help so many others until he calls you home again."

Letters like Eran's enable me to rejoice but also make me realize how important it was for me *and for others* to hold on and to endure the pain.

Several years ago, I attended my first writers' conference in Nashville, Tennessee. One of my stories won an award and I felt pretty good about it. At lunchtime I sat at a table with several people and we introduced ourselves by giving our names, where we were from, and what we were writing. When my turn came I told them I wanted to write about my death and return to earth.

The last one to introduce himself was Rick Shoemaker and he said he was from New Carlisle, Ohio. He spoke about two sentences before he started to cry. Someone put his arms around Rick. Some asked, "What's the matter?"

"It's just been terrible lately in our small town. Five teenagers have died in the space of six months. I'm tired of doing teenagers' funerals. I feel spent. I'm emotionally wiped out trying to encourage people and to try to understand what's going on."

When Rick paused, someone said, "Don Piper was killed in a car wreck himself and he actually went to heaven. He has a great testimony about his experience."

"We can use some of that in New Carlisle," Rick said.

I didn't want to push myself on him, but I saw the genuine hurt and exhaustion Rick felt. "Is there any way I can help? I'll be glad to do whatever I can."

He thanked me and nothing came of it that day, but later he invited me to visit his church.

"In our church we have a family with two sons," he told me. "On their way back from a concert, their car was broadsided by another vehicle and both died instantly." The boys, Jud and Frank Lawler, had been hit by a semi. "The boys were ages twenty-seven and twenty-four and I had been their pastor for nearly twenty years. Losing them was like losing my own children. Long-term pastorates tend to produce such bonds."

He was quite emotional as he told me, "It was one of the most devastating things I've ever dealt with in my life. The parents are reeling in their pain and confusion. In fact, we're all reeling. Could you come and tell us about heaven?"

"I'd be honored to do that," I said.

We set a date and I went to the church. Rick arranged for me to have lunch with the parents after the morning worship. As I expected, the parents were heartbroken. The father talked about his sons, and from everything he said and the reports of others, they genuinely were two incredible kids. The parents tried to make sense of their tragedy. I tried to encourage them and prayed for them. I also felt an incredible burden to try to talk to them about the reality of heaven.

Our lunch lasted almost three hours. "I have two sons and I'm heartbroken just talking to you. I didn't even know your boys and I'm devastated by this tragedy you've endured. I just am. I don't know how you make it, but I can tell you on the authority of the Bible and based on my own experience: Your sons are waiting for you. And I can tell you that you're still here for a reason."

"Well, I don't see what it is," the father said. He was too broken up at that point to think about any purpose.

I spoke to him several times while I was at the church and I could tell he truly struggled.

"I'm going to try to find a purpose—find that new normal you talked about," he said, just before the last service. "I know we'll never be the same. I don't know how long it's going to take."

"I don't either. I really don't," I said. "I can't imagine a greater pain than you've experienced, but you're not alone. A lot of people are pulling for you. Be patient with yourself and trust these words: There's something that God wants you to do that you never would have been able to do if this had not happened."

In 2005, I was privileged to return to First Baptist Church of New Carlisle. What a joy it was to preach in Rick's church again. But before I did, a couple rose to lead in congregational singing. Yes, it was the Lawlers—the parents I had met in my previous visit. She played the piano (one donated by them in memory of their sons, who had been gifted musicians) and he directed the singing. Joy and meaning had returned to their lives. Through their endurance, they are still touching the hearts of others who suffered the same kind of pain.

After I received Rick's permission to tell this story, he sent me more information that I want to include here:

"Shortly before you came to New Carlisle the second time, I was asked to visit a man in Community Hospital in Springfield, Ohio. Although not a Christian, he requested that a pastor come to speak with him about his impending death. I agreed to go. When I entered the room of Jack Rains, his daughter was telling him about a book she had read in which a man had died, gone to heaven, and came back again.

"When she paused, I asked, 'Were you referring to Don Piper?'

"Startled, she said, 'Yes, how did you know?'

"I explained that you were a friend and that you were scheduled to speak at our church again in a few weeks. She wept openly at God's gracious ministry to her broken heart.

"A short time later Jack Rains prayed to receive Christ as his Savior. Not long after that, when I preached Jack's funeral, I shared your testimony. Several who attended that memorial service would later come to hear you. Two or three of that group also came to faith in Christ."

Frequently people say to me, "You're the bravest person I know" or "I just can't believe you overcame all of this." Or, "It's just amazing what you are able to do. The surgeries you had to have, the therapy you had to endure, and how relentless you were with sticking with the therapy. Then there are the times when you don't feel like it, but you get up out of bed and you go answer the call at three o'clock in the morning because somebody needs to see you. There's also the fact that you're willing to go five thousand miles to speak to somebody who needs to know about Jesus."

They interpret that as courageousness or heroic, but I don't feel courageous. I just don't see it as that; it's what I need to do. Maybe courage is a matter of perception. Maybe it's having the fortitude to do the will of God—to hold on and to do what we were made to do. For a long time I didn't know that I was called to share the message that I have.

"This is just the most amazing story: I'm just overwhelmed by this story," people say to me. "I've never heard anything like this."

"It is pretty amazing. It's very real. It really happened this way and I don't recommend getting hit by a big truck so you'll have a good story." I usually follow up by saying, "But if you do get hit by a big truck, you ought to have a good story."

Along with great crisis, great tragedy, great pain, and great suffering are also great opportunities. So if taking those opportunities and doing God's will is an example of courage I guess I'll accept some of that. But I don't feel very heroic.

I could have given up and shriveled up, that's true. And I was tempted to do so. But I never entertained the temptation very long. To entertain such ideas is like allowing sin to intrigue and tantalize us. If we entertain sin long enough it'll camp in our yard and then move inside. I never dwelt on the idea of giving up, and it never occurred to me that I wasn't going to walk again. It apparently occurred to everybody else, but I was utterly determined that I would stand and walk on my own two feet. And eventually I became utterly determined that I was going to make a difference, that I was going to take whatever I had and try to help other people through my experience and insight. I believe it's not what happens to us that matters, it's what we do with what happens to us. And so if that is some cousin to courage, call me courageous.

What I do want to say is this: Regardless of whether I've been courageous, heroic, brave, or anything approaching that, it does take some amount of courage to overcome. I'm of the conviction that in order to move beyond the setbacks and to defeat the difficulty, we have to fight. No matter what our difficulty or our disaster, we have to stand up to it. And we can find the courage to fight if we remember that God is always near us to give us whatever we need to stay with the battle until the end.

I hope people will understand that this grace to hold on isn't an automatic response. It often takes something deep within us— a sense of God's power and love. One of the great sayings I grew up with—and I don't know the author—was this: "God's man is immortal until his work on earth is done." God will enable us to survive to fulfill his purpose for us. I believe this now, and when I was confined to a hospital bed after my accident, it is what kept me going.

I'm not interested in celebrating any courage for whatever I've endured. I am interested in saying to people, "You are going through a terrible time in your life, but it's not your entire life, and it's not the end of your life. It's one part—a terrible, horrible, difficult part—but you'll get past it. It may take strong determination. It may demand the prayer and support of all your friends. It may mean struggles to overcome the desire to quit, but you can make it."

Even though I'm not now nor have I ever been really comfortable with the label of courage, I understand that I had to contribute something to the process. God is still in the miracle business and he worked many miracles in my life. God answered prayers and my return to earth is a testimony to answered prayer. But I did endure, I did hold on.

We have to keep on. We can't just languish and give up. If we believe we are immortal until God has completed his purpose in our lives, we can hold on a little longer.

I have a friend named Stan Cottrell who has had his own share of hard times and one of the things he often says is, "Five minutes. Just hold on for five more minutes."

It's Stan's way of saying what I advocate. God does the miracles and we participate by continuing to fight and not surrender. The next five minutes can make the difference. We can call that courage. But what we call it isn't important. What we do is.

I emphasize this because those I consider the most courageous often don't see themselves that way. For example, during Hurricane Katrina in 2005, the streets of New Orleans flooded. One man was swept downstream and hit a tree. "I held on," he said. "I was scared and too afraid to let go, so I held on." He held on to that tree for nine hours before a helicopter rescued him. He saw it as nothing special; I see it as the courage and the commitment to hold on. To let go is easy; anyone can quit.

Some of the most courageous people I know are those who just get up and go to work every day. What about police officers or firefighters? We can't overlook the heroic teachers in our schools, who give themselves for lower pay than they'd make in another profession, but they do it because it's their purpose in life. Missionaries are courageous people who leave the comforts of their home and immerse themselves in foreign cultures, even those where they're hated because they're Americans.

The world is filled with courageous people. But no matter how we define them, they're the ones who hold on as they face problems and hardships. They may feel inadequate and alone, but they don't let go.

Just hold on.

TWENTY-THREE

Prayer Power

In Paul's great words in Philippians 4, he exhorts, "Do not be anxious about anything, but in everything, by prayer and petition, with thanksgiving, present your requests to God. And the peace of God, which transcends all understanding, will guard your hearts and your minds in Christ Jesus" (Philippians 4:6–7**).

I survived because of prayer. One man, Dick Onarecker, felt God impress on him to pray and he did. He prayed me back to this earth. Many people who heard about my accident prayed for me and the word spread across the country.

I never prayed for my own recovery.

During many of the days and months I spent in the hospital, I wasn't sure I wanted to recover. I was ready at any point for God to take me back to heaven. After my brief visit to heaven, I longed to go back, and I had trouble understanding why God brought me back.

Eventually I realized that God wanted me on earth. And much later, I realized God wanted me to share my story to encourage others and to bring them hope. But before all of that, I had to get to the point where I could pray for a meaningful existence and for direction.

Whenever I was conscious in those early days after the accident, I knew my life had changed drastically—and I struggled to make sense of my life and of the role I would have. That's when I realized I had to find the new normal, even though those aren't the words I used at the time. I used words like *purpose*, *usefulness*, and *adaptation*.

When the accident occurred, I was the youth minister and the minister of education at a Baptist church in Alvin, Texas. It didn't take much thinking for me to realize I couldn't be a youth minister very long and had to seek another position. That work involved a tremendous amount of very intense physical activity, such as camps, retreats, lock-ins, parties; I seemed constantly to be doing something or going somewhere with the youth. Physically I could not keep up with them. I couldn't stay up all night at a lock-in with a bunch of kids.

In those first months after my return, it was more than just not enough energy. I wore the Ilizarov brace—or, as they called it, a fixator—and I was in a wheelchair. Because of the brace, my left leg was straight out and I couldn't move it or lower it.

One time I tried to go to camp with them, and it was a painful ordeal and took too much out of me. Worse than my ordeal, I was more of a burden on the kids than I was a help. They constantly had to take care of me and that wasn't the purpose of going to camp.

I prayed, of course. So do most Christians. I had a regular prayer time, but I never developed what I would have called an intense prayer life until after the accident. That's when I was forced to depend on God for everything.

I believed in prayer, in God, in salvation through Jesus Christ, the Bible—all the things most Christians hold dear. But after I had been in the midst of perfection and total happiness, not only did I want to return to heaven, but I wanted others to go there as well. I felt infused with what some would call a missionary zeal. I had briefly experienced the perfect world and I wanted others to join me there.

I knew the way, as I've already mentioned. More than ever, I wanted to help others find the way before they had to cross their final bridges. Based on the gifts and the physical ability that I still had, I asked God to show me what I was to do next. After much prayer, I decided the next step was to become a pastor.

Along with that decision, the depth and intensity of my prayer life increased. For those of us who go through those hard, painful, and life-changing events as we seek balance—a new normal—prayer becomes indispensable. It became as natural to pray as it does to breathe or talk.

I'm one of those people who needs God to write the words with a fingertip in the sky. I'm not particularly perceptive about God's will or direction. Despite that, I don't want to make a move without being certain of what God has in mind for me. In prayer I asked him to make it absolutely clear to me what he wanted me to do. God usually does that, and I'm grateful.

One of the things I learned in prayer was to think positively—and that means to pray positively. Instead of putting my focus on what was wrong or what might go wrong, I wanted to focus on the right. During my time in the hospital, for example, I stopped asking, "Don't let me get infected again" and instead I thanked God for each day with lessened pain or no new infection.

If we learn to think positively and to pray positively, we learn to act positively. Unless we aggressively pursue the new normal and work toward being upbeat about the outcome, we'll continue to struggle and constantly waffle from highs to lows. If we continue to say, "I can't do that," we probably can't. That's why being positive is so powerful. Once we focus properly, we're open and ready for good things to happen in our lives. Without the right attitude, we won't find a meaningful existence. If, however, we turn to positive prayer, we can become as effective—and perhaps more effective—than we were before. We'll be different. We may be limited in some ways, as I was, but life will take on deeper meaning.

As I prayed my way forward, my life changed. Instead of working exclusively with the youth, I found meaning through my ministry as a pastor to the entire church. I didn't make the choice because I felt youth weren't worthy of my time, but because I could no longer fulfill that role effectively. I had to seek guidance from the Lord to know what I could do effectively.

I also learned that not only must we learn to pray positively, we have to be faithful and systematic in our devotional life. By that I mean it's not just an occasional crying out to God, but a serious, committed, daily, ongoing cry for God's guidance. If we have established a relationship with our Heavenly Father, we have the right to expect him to lead us.

Another lesson I learned is that we must do something besides just ask for guidance. Prayer doesn't end with saying the words. Prayer truly becomes effective when we act by following the guidance we receive when God answers us—*and God will answer us*. One of my friends says, "We need to put legs on our prayers." It's action. It's not sitting and waiting for God to change us or our circumstances. We have to listen to hear God's voice and then act on it.

I've also seen too many people with misdirected prayers. They call out to God asking him to turn back the clock and return things to the way they were before . . . before the accident, before the tragedy, before the loss. But as I've said repeatedly in this book, we can't go back to the past. Praying to go backward is futile and is actually detrimental because it prevents us from moving forward. For example, many times a divorced man or woman has come to my office and wailed, "I want our marriage put back together. I just want life to be the way it used to be."

I don't say much. Even if both husband and wife were able to resolve their differences and come together, life could never be the way it used to be. In the interim period, both have changed. They can pray for a new balance—a new normal—but they won't find it by looking back to the way it used to be.

After my release from the hospital, I dreamed of how life might have been if I had taken the other way home. But I also accepted the fact that I could not undo the past. I focused my prayers on finding how to live with circumstances as they were now. Daily I pleaded for God to show me the way, give me the strength, and uplift my spirit. Our God is a faithful God. He never abandoned me, even when I abandoned hope. And he answered my prayers beyond my wildest dreams.

After my accident, I received a lot of pressure to apply for disability. I certainly qualified. People at the Workmen's Compensation Board said, "You're disabled."

Yes, I could have accepted disability and I seriously considered it, but I suppose I have enough of a fighting spirit that I simply could not apply. Anybody who looked at me would have thought, "This guy will never have any kind of meaningful existence again." *And they could have been correct.* I could have given in and let everyone tell me what I could no longer do. The more I prayed, however, the more convinced I became that I needed to focus on what I could do.

After much prayer and a sense of God's guidance, I took a positive attitude. "I think I can function—not as I did in the past, but I can still function as a minister," I told my family. "My focus will have to be different now. My physical limitations mean I won't be able to do the same activities I did before. I'll do what I can and not worry about what I can't do."

Because I prayed, and because my family and friends prayed, God helped me and I was able to find a way to have a positive attitude. I got busy. I knew that if I was going to function to the best of my new abilities I had to do two things. First, I had to get more education. I attended more conferences on preaching, took additional seminary courses, subscribed to more professional publications, and studied specific ministry resources.

Second, I had to make contacts. I had to let people know what I could do and that I was willing. Most of the people who heard about me wouldn't have known that I wasn't giving up and that I was available.

For too many, it's easier to worry than it is to pray. The great apostle knew that. I quoted Paul at the beginning of this chapter. In Philippians 4, he says not to be anxious about anything. Anxiety isn't the same as worry, but it's pretty close. When you're anxious or worried it's like you're saying, "God, I don't think you're able or interested in taking care of me."

Paul assures his readers that if they push anxiety aside—and we can do that—we can discover peace with God.

As I read and meditated on Philippians 4:6–7, I realized something. We can take everything—every need—to God. I had always known that, of course, but now I knew it by experience. We can pray for ourselves and we can pray for others. I once heard a preacher say, "If anything is big enough to bother you, it's big enough to pray about."

Our praying isn't just to get answers or to see miracles. Our prayers are our connecting point with God. When we pray, we're in fellowship with God. It's an intimate giving of ourselves to God and responding to his overwhelming love. We're saying, "Here's who I am and here are the places where I see needs." And God says, "I know and I care."

And in the midst of all those minor and major problems, we can give thanks. I've written about thanksgiving in another chapter, but I want to add this: When we praise God, in essence we're saying, "I banish worry and anxiety because I see how you have worked in the past. As I pause to remember and to reflect, I'm able to trust you more for the present needs and for the future."

When we pray as Paul describes, he also promises God's peace. He says that God's peace acts like a sentinel who is always on duty—always keeping us feeling safe in God's love.

People sometimes tell me of the outstanding power of prayers because their friends or family members recovered from serious illness. Here's a letter from a woman who praises God for a different kind of answer to her prayer:

"My mother wasn't an easy person to get along with. And that's not just my opinion. She and my father divorced because he couldn't put up with her manipulations and demands. Mom alienated my two siblings and neither of them spoke to her for more than ten years. Two years ago she became extremely ill and it took months for the doctors to correctly diagnose her problem.

"She was unable to take care of herself and, as the oldest sibling, I agreed to take her in—even though my husband wasn't in favor of it. Mom was as demanding as ever. Each day I prayed for God's help. 'Make her well so I can get her out of here, or give me the love and grace I need to take care of her.'

"After I heard Don speak at a church in the Atlanta area, God did something *for me*. I was able to see her as a wounded person. She was in physical pain all the time but I saw that as symptomatic of the internal pain.

"For the first time in my forty-one years of life, I sat down beside my mother and said, 'I don't understand you, but I want to love you. Help me love you.'

"Mom stared at me for a long time before her lips quivered and she finally said, 'I'm sorry. I guess I hate everybody because I hate myself.' I had never heard her speak like that—not ever. She turned her face away from me and wouldn't say anything more. But it was enough and I felt God had answered my prayers.

"A few days later, Mom had a massive coronary and died. I'm sorry Mom and I didn't have time after that conversation to draw close, but I believe God answered me in both ways. I changed and so did Mom. Nowadays when I think of those two years she was with me, I can give thanks to God. I learned to be more patient, to pray more about things that bother me, and to realize that those who come across as mean-spirited individuals also hurt."

God does answer our prayers. He listens to our words and understands our needs. He does take care of us.

God wants us to pray. That's one of the foundations of our faith. Jesus exhorted his followers not to worry but to pray. In the famous Sermon on the Mount, he pointed out that God takes care of the creatures of nature and we're more important than they are.

Prayer is more than asking and receiving—although that's important. When we ask, it shows we depend on God. It declares that we need help to do what we can't do for ourselves. But prayer is also our special communion with our Creator. When we pray— truly pray—we open ourselves to God. I'm going to use an old-fashioned word that's still powerful: We have *fellowship* with him. Prayer draws us closer and makes us more open to the quiet voice of the Holy Spirit.

But we can't pray and hear God if worries and troubles fill our hearts and minds. Just before his death, Jesus spent the evening with his disciples and he prepared them for his leaving. "Do not let your hearts be troubled. Trust in God; trust also in me" (John 14:1†).

Some people can banish worry by themselves, but most of us need other people in those difficult and troubled times. Sometimes we need others because we can't do anything for ourselves.

A man in Atlanta was robbed, shot in the chest and leg, and spent weeks in the hospital before he recovered. "I couldn't pray for myself," he said. "I just didn't care if I lived or died. In fact, I suppose I hoped I would die. I was tired of the agony, of the pain."

Three years later, he still endures a lot of physical pain from the gunshot wounds, but he said, "My church carried me through the process. They prayed for me when I couldn't."

I understand him because that's also my story. Sometimes we're so beat up from life or gunshot wounds or car accidents, we have no strength to care about ourselves. That's exactly how I felt. That's why I often jokingly say, "I'm back on earth by popular demand. People prayed for me when I couldn't pray for myself." That's powerful.

When we pray for others, it has a strong effect. The Bible says it this way: "The earnest prayer of a righteous person has great power and produces wonderful results" (James 5:16b**). The writer follows with an example of Elijah, the great prophet. "Elijah was as human as we are, and yet when he prayed earnestly that no rain would fall, none fell for the next three and a half years! Then when he prayed again, the sky sent down rain and the earth began to yield its crops" (Verses 17–18).

I'm delighted that I can rely on others—as I did during those early days of recovery and as I still do today. I couldn't pray for my survival; I left that up to caring people, and they didn't disappoint me.

Eventually I recovered enough that I could pray for myself. One thing I did and continue to do: I asked people to pray for me specifically. I told them exactly how I wanted them to pray and they became my prayer partners.

I learned to covenant with others to pray for specific things.

That's a wonderful example of the body of Jesus Christ functioning together. We join our hearts in a common purpose. I think that pleases God.

Because of my positive experience with covenant praying, I urge others to do that same thing. For more than twenty years, my cowriter has practiced what he calls "contract praying." When people speak to him about needs and ask him to pray, he asks two questions: First: "For what do you want me to pray? Be as specific as you can." Second, he asks, "For how long do you want me to pray?"

When we hold up one another, we practice the biblical principle. Jesus sent his first disciples out by twos. There's wisdom in that because one can lift up the other in moments of trouble or hardship.

We also need to consider support groups. Some people have a fear of sharing intimate details, but that's part of the issue of trust. It's part of learning to share with one another. I don't suggest blabbing about everything in our lives, but often in support groups when a person opens up, it's exactly what another person needs to hear.

One woman told me that she was in a prayer group and finally opened up and told them about some personal things. "It was hard, but I did it." She said when she finished, another woman started to cry. "For weeks I've prayed about the same thing. I thought I was the only one who felt that way. When I came here tonight I prayed. I asked the Lord to help me. You have been my answer to prayer."

I believe we all need support groups of some kind. Some older adults remind me of the days when they went to church on Wednesday nights and spent at least half of the services in prayer for specific needs. We don't see much of that these days, but I think the principle is right.

Another thing about support groups is that it works both ways—as we support, we're supported. As we give, we also receive. As we pray for others, God smiles on us and connects us more closely with each other.

TWENTY-FOUR

I Have This Confidence

The fact that I have survived and that I can walk on my own makes a difference to me for many reasons. First, I'm obviously delighted because I can move on my own. Many times people have seemed genuinely surprised and quite excited when they see me walk into the building and up to the platform all on my own. They expected me to show up in a wheelchair or they assumed I'd have to be assisted up onto the stage.

Sometimes I feel as if I need to be assisted, especially after a long day, but I'm not going to quit doing it on my own as long as I can make it. It's not a matter of pride. It's because I want other people to know that they can make it through life's hardships. They can overcome the horrible events in their lives. We may not be able to do all the things we once did, but we can do more if we don't give up.

I recently thought about a well-accepted axiom in the business world. It's the 20-60-20 rule. Whenever there is a significant change in any business, 20 percent of the people enthusiastically grab on to the change. Another 20 percent resist the change just because it's change; no matter how much reasoning goes on, they're closed to the idea of something different. About 60 percent of the people are in the middle. They don't know which way to go. It's that 60 percent I want to touch, and to them I want to say, "You can do it. You can overcome the problems of your lives." I want them to know, as I do, that God works in our lives and will be with us always.

As I've mentioned over and over again, I find great comfort in Paul's letter to the Philippians. After his greeting, he wrote, "In all my prayers for all of you, I always pray with joy because of your partnership in the gospel from the first day until now, being confident of this, that he who began a good work in you will carry it on to completion until the day of Christ Jesus" (Philippians 1:4–6[†]).

He rejoices because the people of the city of Philippi have faithfully given themselves to partner with the apostle from the time they became believers, and Paul sees this as God at work within them. He tells them he is confident that God will continue to be with them, will never leave them, will remain with them until they cross the final bridge that leads to heaven's gate.

God at work in us is a powerful concept, one we don't stress much today. I constantly hear people speak of believing in Jesus Christ and I'm delighted when I do. But the proof—the real test—comes to light when we look at their lives. When people truly believe, Jesus guides their actions and empowers them to do great things. They not only talk the talk, but they walk the walk.

We need to have confidence that the power of God will work in us and enable us to accomplish the seemingly impossible. It is this confidence that enables me to continue traveling all over the world sharing my message. In fact, it is this confidence that even enables me to get out of bed each day. I trust that God works in me and through me. He can work in you as well.

Paul also writes of that confidence in God in his letter to Timothy. Paul acknowledges that he was called to be a messenger of God's Good News, an apostle, and a teacher, and he writes, "That is why I am suffering as I am. Yet I am not ashamed, because I know whom I have believed, and am convinced that he is able to guard what I have entrusted to him for that day" (2 Timothy 1:12†).

In that verse he spoke of what he had entrusted to God. The Greek word he uses is *paratheke*. It carries the idea of safekeeping. When people wanted to keep something safe, they gave it to a person or took it to the temple. In the ancient world, the person who kept the *paratheke* took on a sacred responsibility. Paul had made his deposit by faith in Jesus Christ. That is, he entrusted both his life and work to God. That was the confidence about which the apostle wrote. He staked his life on the faithfulness of God.

As we read the writings of Paul and witness all his sufferings, we never see him doubt or question. He knew God was with him—he knew with the kind of certainty I know about heaven. This is the same man who assured the Romans, "And I am convinced that nothing can ever separate us from God's love. Neither death nor life, neither angels nor demons, neither our fears for today nor our worries about tomorrow—not even the powers of hell can separate us from God's love" (Romans 8:38**).

He didn't write from theory; he wrote from experience.

I want to share a sad story with you and I don't think this situation is totally unique. The woman writes:

"I've been a Christian since I was eight years old. I never questioned that I'd go to heaven because that's what I'd been taught. But a lot of changes have taken place in my life during the past two years and I don't know where I'm going. I believe in the Lord, but I didn't do much living to honor that relationship. I'm embarrassed to write all this, but there was nothing in my life that would show an outsider that I was a believer. Okay, I went to church two or three times a month, but that's about all.

"In the past two years, everything in my life crashed. My world caved in and I felt lost and abandoned by God. My husband had a stroke at age forty-one—and he has limited mobility and is unable to work. I had a short-lived affair with a coworker and felt so guilty I broke it off. Five weeks ago, our only daughter was walking across the street and a distracted woman drove through a red light, hit her, and almost killed her. She's fine now, but for two days she hovered between life and death.

"Several people from the church where I occasionally attended came to me and prayed with me and encouraged me. They arranged to help me with the care of my husband so I could go back to work. (I have two sons in elementary school.)

"But the best part is that I'm active in the church again. I've turned to God in a stronger way than ever. I want to serve God with all my heart.

"I just have one question: Does God really accept me back again? One of my friends said that I could never be as close to God as I was once—back in the early days of my marriage. Have I been so awful and sinful that God will accept me but, you know, sort of hold me at arm's length? I don't want to go back to the old ways, and I've discovered the joy of serving God. I pray regularly, and I'd like to do more at church—but is that all right?"

I didn't have any kind of great wisdom for her, but one thing I could say is God loves her and loves her enough that he'll never stop loving her.

The book of Hebrews says this: " 'Never will I leave you; never will I forsake you.' So we say with confidence, 'The Lord is my helper, I will not be afraid. . . .' " (13:5–6†).

I went on to tell her that not only was it wrong that she could never be as close, but the way was now open for her to be closer. Before she believed and knew God loved her. Now God has proven that love—God has accepted her when she felt totally unworthy of acceptance.

She wrote me months later and thanked me. "I was so discouraged. I was ready to give up because I wanted more of God and didn't know if God wanted me—really wanted me—to be close. It seems silly now, but that's the kind of mess I was in."

I can say to her what Paul wrote to the Philippians about "being confident of this, that he who began a good work in you will carry it on to completion until the day of Christ Jesus" (Philippians 1:6). In fact, I thought that God used the awful mess in her life to remind her of his presence and his love. God sent those church members to her.

As I thought about what Paul wrote to his disciples, I realized that he wanted to comfort them and teach them to be joyful, regardless of what went on in their lives. When he wrote about joy because of their partnership in the gospel from the first day until the present, it wasn't just their material support—their gifts to him that he was talking about. He was also referring to their sympathy, their prayers, and their witness of faithfulness in their own church.

Because of their behavior—not just their words—Paul expressed his assurances that they would continue in the same fruitful activity until they died or Christ returned. That confidence is based not on their faithfulness as much as on the grace and faithfulness of God.

Because I believe in divine faithfulness, I can talk about it and point out how it has worked in my life. One of the great blessings of having experienced the reality of heaven is that I have total confidence in the promises contained in the Bible. I was there. I know they are true.

TWENTY-FIVE

Why Didn't God Heal Me Completely?

"Why didn't God heal you?" the woman asked. "After your wonderful trip to heaven and back, why did God stop then? You didn't have any brain damage or any internal injuries. That's a miracle. If God did that for you, why didn't he finish the job?"

I hear that question occasionally and I think it deserves an answer.

The most basic, honest answer I can give is this: I don't know.

I've certainly thought about it often enough. I truly wish God had given me a healthy body like I had before I drove across that bridge. I don't like the pain and tiredness and the struggles just to do the normal things in life.

Do I believe God could heal me? Absolutely.

Would I like to be healed? Does that question even deserve an answer? I'd love to leap up and down, bend over, take long walks the way I used to, or run down the street. I would like to ride a bike again, play tennis and golf, or go snow skiing. Perhaps even more, I wish I could squat down and look a child directly in the eye or straighten out my permanently crooked left arm so I could play catch with my grandchild.

Fully clothed, I look like any middle-aged man. But those clothes mask a permanently mangled man.

Occasionally I meet wonderful, caring people who come to my meetings and they tell me they believe God wants to heal me. I'm all for that. They lay hands on me and pray fervently for a miracle of healing to take place.

It's happened many times and after they've prayed, I'm no better. In fact, I actually feel a little worse because they're so genuinely sincere. I'm touched by their compassion. My healing hasn't happened; it will probably never happen.

Even though I write those words, I also want to be open to the possibility that the Lord might send me another miracle and heal my body. I don't doubt God's ability to heal me completely or people's ability to pray. I'm alive today because many prayed for me. God wanted me to live. His purpose includes that I would live with these disabilities in order to bless others. So in the years since 1989, I've learned to adjust and to form a new normal in my life.

Why didn't God heal me? Why did God let me walk up to the gates of heaven, hear the heavenly music, and send me back? I could just as easily ask (and I have) why God didn't let me stay. I didn't *choose* to return. No one asked me, but godly people prayed for me. I also want to make it clear that although I have no death wish, I'm absolutely ready right now to cross that final bridge and to enter into the endless, perfect bliss that I briefly experienced.

But I came back from heaven and I came back with a mangled body. I have several theories on the reason and I'll share them.

First, we pay a price for everything we get in life. If we turn to Jesus Christ, it means we leave our old way of life and often our friends. Some of those friends—especially if we've known them a long time before we turned our lives around—reject us, taunt us, or work against us.

As a pastor I used to hear those stories. A twenty-five-year-old man became a believer and left a live-in relationship with a woman. She didn't understand (or didn't want to understand) and spread stories that he was really gay and physically abusive. When he told me about it, he was deeply hurt, but he also knew that he couldn't win by retaliating. (He did write her a letter in which he said he was sorry she was hurt, but that he could not continue in that lifestyle. In this case, she stopped spreading stories about him.)

For gifted individuals to become outstanding at a musical instrument or sports, it means they have to focus on what they want to accomplish and turn away from fun activities that their friends engage in.

I believe my remaining physical disability is the price I paid for the heavenly visit. I can say that because of my understanding of the apostle Paul's experience. I don't mean to compare myself with that great saint, but I believe we both had an earth-to-heaven-to-earth experience.

Previously I referred to his experience. In 2 Corinthians 11:16–33, he listed the persecution he endured. In Chapter 12 he says (but we think he referred to himself): "I know a man in Christ who fourteen years ago was caught up to the third heaven. Whether it was in the body or out of the body I do not know— God knows" (Verse 2[†]).

One translation reads this way: "[But I do know] that I was caught up to paradise and heard things so astounding that they cannot be expressed in words. . . ." (Verse 4**). That's exactly how I feel about heaven. I have tried to talk about it, but I can't begin to make clear my experience. That's why I resonate so clearly with the apostle.

I mentioned previously we pay a price for everything. Paul paid a price for that heavenly experience. "I don't want anyone to give me credit beyond what they can see in my life or hear in my message, even though I have received such wonderful revelations from God" (Verse 6b–7).

He went on to say that he was given a thorn in the flesh,[7] a messenger of Satan to torment him (Verse 7, most translations). No one knows whether it was a physical ailment (as is most generally accepted) or some kind of spiritual torment. The point is that Paul had something in his life that constantly tormented him so that he didn't become conceited (or "puffed up" in some versions).

Paul didn't like what happened. He says, "Three times I pleaded with the Lord to take it away from me" (Verse 8†). In his case, God did answer and said, "My grace is sufficient for you, for my power is made perfect in weakness" (Verse 9a). That was enough for Paul because he grasped a powerful truth: When he was weak, he relied more fully on God for strength. Had he been physically perfect, why would he need to call on God for daily strength?

Second, God is sovereign and he doesn't have to explain. Rather than resent God's refusal to heal, Paul praised the Lord. He under-

---

[7] The Greek word is *skolops*, which can mean a thorn, but Paul probably meant a stake that twisted in his body. One form of Roman death was to impale criminals on a sharp stake.

stood the reason for his continuing disability. I'm not quite as spiritual as Paul, but I certainly see that element. God gave me a powerful privilege—I saw heaven. I experienced the reality of heaven. I can talk about it and share my story with people—and I do.

Third, I believe the reason God didn't heal me is for me to have the memory—the full memory. Each day when I start to get up, my body wants to rebel and fight me. Especially when I'm on the road, I feel so weary it's almost a miracle for me to get myself out of bed.

That's one part of the memory. The other part is the inexpressible joy of what I experienced during those ninety minutes in heaven. It was real and remains real. I believe my physical pain helps the memory to remain strong.

That may sound odd, but I believe what I write here. Because I have to call out to God for strength every day, I'm reminded of the reason I'm back here on earth. Paul wrote, "Therefore I will boast all the more gladly about my weaknesses, so that Christ's power may rest on me. That is why, for Christ's sake, I delight in weaknesses, in insults, in hardships, in persecutions, in difficulties. For when I am weak, then I am strong" (Verse 9b–10).

Memory of my experience in heaven stays sharp because the pain reminds me. As I feel the weakness and the pain, I also retain powerful memories of the reality of heaven.

Fourth, I believe I can impact others with my disability. When I talk to people in pain or hear from those who have read my books, many of them know about my physical problems. "I felt as if you spoke just for me" is something I hear a lot. I smile because I believe that's my purpose.

Some tell me that I've inspired them to keep trying and not to give up. Others tell me that I've enabled them to accept their situations and to realize that God is truly with them.

I've received e-mails from people who have contemplated suicide because of their accidents. One man had become addicted to methamphetamine and fell from the third floor of his apartment building. His accident left him in agony and permanently paralyzed. "I was tired of the pain. I just wanted it to be over," he wrote. He listened to my CD about heaven and told my cowriter, "If Don Piper can endure, I can endure. I'll never walk again," he said, "but Don has helped me realize that I'm alive. I'm also off 'the ice' and have experienced the love of Jesus Christ."

Because I limp to the podium to speak and fight exhaustion by the end of the evening, I believe my message has a greater impact. My audience can sense a little of what I went through. I don't go around showing my physical scars; most people don't want to see them anyway, but they're there.

I know that my life has meaning for me—more meaning than I ever understood before. But my life also has meaning for others. I'm the living proof of the reality of heaven. Despite the thorn in my own flesh, I'm grateful that God has given me the immense task—and great pleasure—of offering hope to others.

TWENTY-SIX

Was It Worth It?

"Was it worth it?" The man's eyes asked as intently as his voice. "After all you went through and after seeing you in person, I have to hear the answer to that question."

I answered him and I'll share that because others have asked the same question. Before I answer directly, however, I want to point out what I consider the background for my response.

To begin with, despite the pain, the surgeries, the lengthy rehabilitation process, I have never doubted the reality of heaven or the reality of my experience. It wasn't some mystical kind of happening or a vivid dream. It was genuine. In fact, in some ways, it felt more real than life on this earth.

I had crossed the bridge from this world to heaven. That didn't make me perfect or give me enormous wisdom. The experience did enable me to rethink my motives and priorities. Over a lengthy period, I learned to think from a heavenly perspective. My thinking gradually shifted and now I make choices based on their eternal consequences.

That experience that began on the Texas bridge has taught me many lessons. I want to share two of those lessons.

First, one of the greatest lessons for me was that God never intended any of us to live independently. I had been the pastor, the educated theologian. I was there for others, but I didn't need others. I liked other people, but I was able to take care of myself. But after my return from heaven, one of the great changes was to accept a reality: I needed other people. I was no longer only the helper; I had also become the helped.

It took me a long time to realize it, but I needed help. I needed the two men who drove the ambulance, the doctors, and the nurses. In the hospital, visitors brought me magazines, newspapers, music cassettes. They filled me with milkshakes and fruit. I needed incredible amounts of help after I got out of the hospital, everything from the physical therapists to patient family members to praying churches to everything else. People helped me get past the events of the bridge.

For most of my Christian experience I had read the verses that tell us that Christians are all parts of a mystical body and that Christ is the head. In 1 Corinthians 12:12–31, the apostle Paul writes a lengthy passage about this very topic to emphasize the unity of God's people. He states clearly, "Now you are the body of Christ, and each one of you is a part of it" (Verse 27†).

I knew the teachings of the Bible—I had quoted such words many times. But I hadn't applied them to myself. I had always been the helper; I hadn't been in a situation where I had to depend on others because I couldn't do things for myself. It wasn't an easy lesson for me to learn, but it was an important one. God has always meant for us to be in a reciprocal relationship. Now I help others and am grateful that I can be of service. I receive the benefits of others helping me, and in accepting help enable others to experience the fulfillment that service brings.

We all need each other. Nobody really makes it alone in this life. Sometimes it's more obvious. If we see a woman pushing her husband in a wheelchair, that's obvious he needs her. But maybe she also needs to be needed. The reality is that we need each other in hundreds of ways.

Without exception, every one of us needs others. Not only do we need shoulders on which to lay our heads, but we also need arms to embrace us in our joy. If all believers are part of the body of Christ, that image is to show our common mutuality and dependence.

Second, we have to ask each other for help. That's not easy. For years, I think I expected people to read my mind and to know what I needed even without my saying so.

One desperate man called me and said, "I've got a gun to my head right now. What can I do? I don't want to kill myself but I don't want to live this way anymore."

That was a cry of desperation. From a theological perspective, it was also a way of saying, "I'm part of the same body you are and I need your help."

The man and I spoke for a long time. I didn't solve his problems, but I was able to encourage him and he promised he would get professional help and also call his pastor. Before we hung up I told him how courageous I thought he was. He started to protest but I told him that one of the bravest things we can do is admit we need help.

When I talk with discouraged people I plead with them to accept help to get off the bridge—to move on—and to ask for help to make something of their lives. I say, "You had a train wreck.

You've lost your job or your husband walked out on you or your kids are addicted to drugs. I'm sorry." (And I really am sorry when I hear such stories.) "But don't just sit on the bridge and get hit again. You need to get up and move. And if you can't do it on your own, reach out and ask someone to help you up. Ask your spouse, your friend, your father, your mother, your pastor, or even some guy who died, went to heaven, and came back."

Now that I've said all that, I want to return to the question: "Would you trade being hit by a big truck for what you experienced in heaven? Was it worth it?"

I'll respond to the first question: No, I wouldn't make the trade if I had the choice and I have two reasons for writing that. First, I didn't have the choice. And it has already happened. God made that choice for me to visit heaven and to return. My decision was to decide what I would do with my experience.

Second, I fully expected to see heaven anyway, just not quite that soon. I honestly wasn't curious about what heaven looked like or how I'd feel once I was there. As a serious Christian, I tried to live each day so that I could say the words of the apostle Paul before he died: "I'm about to die, my life an offering on God's altar. This is the only race worth running. I've run hard right to the finish, believed all the way. All that's left now is the shouting—God's applause!" (2 Timothy 4:7–8***).

I also have to say that the heavenly journey gave me a powerful assurance that heaven *is* real. I suppose that's the difference between knowing it's real and experiencing its reality. I could never, never find adequate words to express what I experienced. Even though I had no doubts about the reality of heaven before, all my senses came alive and I stood in the midst of total perfection.

Not only did the heavenly journey give me a greater measure of assurance, I can unhesitatingly assure others of the reality. "I've been there," I can say and say with total honesty, "and it's perfect."

The second question is, "Was it worth it?" Would I really want to go back through all that pain and physical suffering just to have that glimpse? Because I already knew where I was headed, I can't give a 100 percent "yes" answer to that question. On the other hand, I can say it has been worth what I went through because of the opportunities to help hurting and hopeless people. I would never otherwise have had the opportunity to speak to hundreds of thousands of people. From the perspective of ministry—of service for Jesus Christ—how could I not say it was worth it?

At the same time, I don't like to answer that question because it really doesn't matter whether it was worth it. It's a reality. I went to heaven and I'm back and I'm able to speak to people to share my story.

Here's how I've chosen to answer the question: *It must be worth it to God.* He sent me back and he gave me a purpose for living despite my pain.

I waffle on this question because I sense the question isn't really about me, but it's about the people who ask. They're people who hurt—people who are confused and discouraged—and life seems awful for them. When they ask about my pain and whether I think it has been worth it, I often wonder if the real question is this: "Are my sufferings now worth it just to go to heaven when I die?" The pain, the suffering, the hardship, the difficulties—are they worth it for the payoff at the end and to be used by God?

If people hurt or are in pain, that's where they are right now. I like to throw it back to them. Forget about what's up ahead. What about now? What about your life right at this moment? Do you want to live in this place of despair and despondency? Do you want to live where you feel pitiful, pathetic, or useless?

We already know the answer. We don't want to live that kind of sad and empty life.

But just to say those words isn't enough. We have to cross over the bridge from suffering to meaning. No matter how bad our lives, we can find meaning and purpose in them. We can move into a meaningful existence.

I receive a number of e-mails and phone calls from people who help me realize that no matter what pain and suffering I've gone through, it has been worth it all for the encouragement others have received.

For instance, Donna Lawson wrote: "Your story helped me talk to my mother, as she lay on her deathbed. I read your book about a week and half before she died. During her last hours, I told her of your experience. I was able to assure her that as soon as she died, she would be in heaven, and she would see my father (who died three years earlier) and other relatives. They would escort her into the gates of heaven, into the presence of God.

"Your experience helped her not to be afraid. More than anything, I didn't want her to be afraid to go. Her last hours were peaceful, and knowing what to expect helped her. She died last week.

"As painful as your life has been, I'm grateful that you have shared your story. Because of that you helped my mother prepare to meet Jesus."

Here's my final thought about the questions: If we see heaven as just a place to go, it's probably not worth our suffering. But if we think of heaven as the place of perfection—a place without injustice, discrimination, anger, and worry—why wouldn't it be worth it?

The apostle Paul answered that question when he wrote to the Romans. He wrote to believers who were persecuted and despised for their faith. To them he wrote, "If we are to share his glory, we must also share his suffering. Yet what we suffer now is nothing compared to the glory he will reveal to us later" (Romans 8:17b–18**).

TWENTY-SEVEN

The Final Bridge

I started this book by saying it wasn't about my journey *to* heaven, but it's about my journey back *toward* heaven. It's a journey we all take, but we don't all end up at the same destination. That's the one significant decision we must make before we approach the final transition.

Many of us think about crossing that final bridge—especially when we become ill or we lose a loved one. I wish I could help people think about heaven every day instead of only at points of crisis. Part of the reason I've written this book is to urge everyone to think about that final bridge in their lives. We never know when we'll cross over.

I certainly didn't know I would die; I had absolutely no warning. I was living the best way I knew how when the eighteen-wheeler ended my life on earth. After less than two hours, God sent me back, and I believe my purpose in returning is to tell people about the reality of my experience. Because I've been to heaven, I've had a taste of what lies ahead. Like many others, I am preparing myself for that final crossing—where I'll experience endless joy and eternal peace.

I want that for me; I want that for everyone. But how do I share the joys of heaven with people who haven't been there? That's a question I often ask myself. I don't know the answer except to tell my story and hope they'll understand. Some do understand—as much as a person can who receives a secondhand message. Despite the defects of the messenger, they grasp the message.

I don't know everything about heaven—I got only as far as the gate—but I know enough to say that not only is heaven real, but it surpasses anything our minds can possibly conceive.

As I write this book, I'm aware that some readers may feel they're not worthy of heaven. They feel they're too bad or too sinful, they wasted too much of their lives, or they're not good enough for God to want them. They may feel they've done too many wrong things or failed God too many times. *That's totally wrong.* It's the sinful ones, the people who have failed and need help, that God seeks for heavenly occupancy. Heaven is for the imperfect so they can become perfect. (The truth is, we're all imperfect.)

The Bible says again and again that Jesus didn't come for those who are already holy. Instead, his mission was and is to reach for those who know they've failed.

Jesus told a parable about two men. The first man was a religious leader and the other a tax collector (a despised occupation). The story appears in Luke 18:9–14. The religious leader bragged to God about his holy behavior; the other man "would not look up to heaven, but beat his breast and said, 'God, have mercy on me, a sinner.'" Jesus said that the second man rather than the first was justified (or made right) with God.

God's hand stretches toward those who are aware of their need for help. The heavenly hand reaches down to us long before we reach up.

Here's how John, the beloved disciple of Jesus, said it: "If we claim we have no sin, we are only fooling ourselves and not living in the truth. But if we confess our sins to him, he is faithful and just to forgive us our sins and to cleanse us from all wickedness" (1 John 1:8–9**).

If you're imperfect, if you've failed, heaven is for you.

I urge you to get ready, because each of us must cross that final bridge. *The crossing isn't a choice; the destination is.*

In the first chapter I said that I had made a decision at age sixteen. That's when I surrendered my life to Jesus Christ. Call the experience by any number of names: *being born again, born anew, converted,* or *being saved.* The terminology isn't important. What is important is to make a heavenly reservation. And that's all it takes—reserving *your* space in God's eternal paradise.

In Evangelical churches, it's often said, "Heaven is a prepared place for a prepared people," and it's true. No one arrives there accidentally. None of us gets inside unless our name has already been permanently written in the Book of Life. The good news is that Jesus offers the invitation to everyone and each of us can make a reservation. It's simply a matter of admitting our need for divine help. When we acknowledge that we can't save ourselves (and most of us can hardly improve ourselves), that's when we're ready to make our reservation.

But the message I want to share isn't just about our eternal destiny. The message is also that we can enjoy a full, rich life right now. Because we know the ultimate end, we can live better lives in the interim. If we're believers, it doesn't matter what troubles strike or how difficult our situations. God helps us in our daily struggles and gives us the assurance that our eternal future is settled.

God wants you to join me and thousands of others in heaven.

I want to make three points about how to get there:

First, the Bible says that no one is good enough and that every one of us fails. (That's why we call ourselves sinners. The word *sin* is from a Greek archery term that means to miss the mark—the center of the target.) In the third chapter of Romans, the apostle Paul quotes liberally from Psalm 14 to make it clear that no one is worthy or good enough to gain access to God's eternal presence. (See Romans 3:10–18, and especially verse 23.)

Second, once we realize our need, we must turn to the One who makes it possible to enter the heavenly gates. "Jesus said, 'Come to me, all you who are weary and burdened, and I will give you rest'" (Matthew 11:28,†). Jesus also told his followers that he was the way to heaven. (See John 14:6.)

Third, we need to believe that Jesus told us the truth. We need to be able to say, "I believe." Paul wrote, ". . . the gift of God is eternal life in Christ Jesus our Lord" (Romans 6:23b). To the Ephesians he wrote that we are saved or set apart for heaven through our faith ". . . not from yourselves, it is the gift of God—not by works, so that no one can boast" (Ephesians 2:8b–9).

It's that simple. I made the decision at age sixteen. But it doesn't matter if you're twenty-six, forty-six, or eighty-six. Age isn't the issue; the decision is what counts. It's the decision millions have made; it's the decision God wants each of us to make.

That bridge I crossed at age sixteen changed my life: From that moment on, I knew where I was headed. When I crossed that bridge in 1989, it was no accident that I went immediately to the gates of heaven. *I went to heaven because I had prepared for heaven.*

I didn't live every moment from age sixteen to thirty-eight thinking about eternity. I tried to focus on living a life that honored the God I had promised to serve. The real proof of our relationship to Jesus Christ is in the way we live on this earth.

I also want to point out that many people fail—even good, sincere, and dedicated Christians. That's why the Bible constantly offers forgiveness. God is eager to forgive us when we fail at any point along the way, and he wants to pick us up and point us in the right direction. It's the intent of our hearts that God sees, not perfect behavior.

Life has a final bridge that everyone must cross. And now is the time to prepare for our final event on this earth.

"We will probably never meet personally in this lifetime," wrote Alice Eversole in an e-mail, "but I know that I will see you in heaven." She also wrote, "Until then, I want you to know about a 'God-incidence' that got me through the recent loss of my precious mother.

"A close friend and I spent the weekend with mutual dear friends at their cottage at a lake in northeastern Indiana. When I got up that Sunday morning and went out to the enclosed front porch to greet my friends, the television was on to the Coral Ridge Church service with Dr. D. James Kennedy. He announced that his guest that morning was Don Piper, who had gone to heaven for ninety minutes and returned to life because God had more for him to do before he could stay.

"I sat down on the couch and listened with great attention.

My mother had developed dementia and we had had to put her in a nursing home last February, because the burden of caring for her became too great. I knew that her remaining days on this earth were limited and I wanted so much to know more about her next home. What an indescribable peace came over me as I listened to you describe heaven and your experience there.

"Two weeks ago, she fell in the nursing home and broke her left wrist. Due to complications from that, the anesthetic, and other internal problems, she went downhill steadily over the next nine days. A dear friend brought me your book and I began to read about what heaven was like. The next day I sat next to her bed and told her I loved her and that it was all right for her to go home to be with Jesus.

"I was reading your book when I looked over and saw her take her last breath. What a comfort your book has been to me as we said our earthly good-byes."

As I read Alice's e-mail, I thought of her dying mother and the wonderful privilege of the daughter to be there at such a peaceable passing. If we could choose the way to die, most of us would probably like to lie in our own bed surrounded by loved ones. They would tell us how much they loved us and embrace us before we quietly pass away. I've been at the bedside of a few people who have died like that. It's beautiful—a holy transition from life to greater life.

But we don't get to choose. In reality, sometimes death is extremely ugly, horrifying, and painful. We can't make that choice, but we can choose the way we live. We can live each day with grace and dignity, with an assurance that we're going to be in a better place.

When my wife and I and our children talk on the telephone with my parents we always say at the end of the conversation, "I love you." It's not that we didn't say that before the wreck—because we did. But since those days, we've become mindful that we may never have the opportunity to say it again.

Because of what happened to me on the bridge over Lake Livingston, saying "I love you" carries more importance than it ever did. That's not to sound fatalistic, but we know—and no one knows it better than I do—that the end can come at any minute. We need to be prepared.

I look forward to that transition. I can't choose the time or the place of my death, but I can choose how I cross over that final bridge. I don't know how or when it will happen, but here's one simple thing I want and for which I pray: I want to be a faithful witness of God's love and grace and to die in a positive way.

The nineteenth-century evangelist Dwight L. Moody was supposed to have said something like this: "One day you will read in the paper that I died. Don't believe a word of it: I'll be more alive than ever."

One of the great metaphors the church has used to talk about death is that of crossing the Jordan River. They don't refer to a bridge, but I like to think that crossing the Jordan, for believers, means we cross over into the heaven that will be greater than anything we can possibly imagine.

Heaven *is* real. I know because I've experienced that reality. Someday I will cross the final bridge and I'll meet those same people again at the gate. They'll usher me into the presence of Jesus

Christ. I'm ready and I want everyone to be ready. I want everyone to cross that final bridge with the assurance of a reserved space in heaven.

When I sign books, I always write, *See you at the gate.* That's been the focus of my life in the years since my brief trip to heaven.

If you are searching, may you make the right choice. Whether you die by disease or accident, please be ready. If you haven't done so, please make your reservation.

And someday, I hope to meet *you* at the gate.

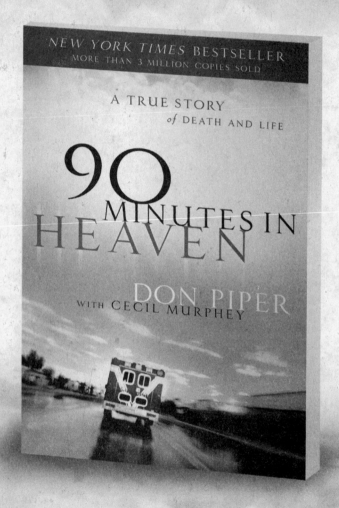